They all called it
TROPICAL

True tales of the Romantic Everglades, Cape Sable, and the Florida Keys

By Charles M. Brookfield and Oliver Griswold

D1636695

Historical Association of Southern Florida
Miami, Florida
Ninth Edition
1985

ISBN 0-935761-01-2
Library of Congress Catalog Card Number: 85-81582

Foreword

Everglades National Park is often described as a unique biological area featuring colorful wildlife and unusual plants. Until now, the human history of the park and its environs has been almost totally neglected. Perhaps this avoidance has stemmed from the fact that history's pages are not splashed with stories of great battles or famous civilizations which rose and fell in the brooding vastness of the Everglades. Its history is one of people—individuals or small groups—who have dared to face one of the strangest environments in the New World. By dugout canoe, stately galleon, sparkling little sharpie sailboat, modern cabin cruiser, or wading on foot, they have come and gone. Some of their "tracks" shall forever be hidden in the timeless Everglades.

"Goin' to th' Cape" does not mean that someone is merely planning a trip to that geographical location at the southern tip of the United States mainland known as Cape Sable. He might be going many miles from there, but "th' Cape" is symbolic of a general area of sub-tropical wilderness where a man is completely on his own. Thus, this "Cape Sable Story" is more than the tale of a beach along the Gulf of Mexico. It tells about those who went "to th' Cape" in the figurative sense as well as those who reached the Cape of Sands itself.

In 1947, the people of the State of Florida presented Everglades National Park to the nation. Stimulated by reports of post-war despoliation of Everglades resources, the State Legislature voted funds and land transfers which made this, our 28th national park, possible. Much of the area will always remain a watery wilderness to be reached only by boat. The existing maintained road, Route 27, from Homestead and Florida City, will be the only access route for some time, although the Florida Keys can be seen from Route 1, the Overseas Highway, and a cross section of the open Everglades is visible by crossing the Tamiami Trail. National Audubon Society Tours from 143 N.E. Third Ave., Miami are the best way for reaching remote areas of the park for the present and near future.

The Park is administered by the National Park Service of the United States Department of the Interior with offices at Homestead, Florida.

Daniel B. Beard,
First Superintendent
Everglades National Park

Introduction

The authors of this book have gone a long way to fulfill a need which has existed in this section of Florida, almost since the beginning.

They have successfully undertaken to answer the hundreds of questions of our visitors, and to confirm or adjust the beliefs of our residents as to:

The background of this amazing area, its development, its history, its romance and its people.

They introduce the reader to some of those who have made outstanding contributions to its progress. This volume highlights the human history of the Everglades National Park area and the adjacent Florida Keys. It reveals little-known facts of the drama enacted about Cape Sable and other sections of this stranger-than-fiction land.

Charles M. Brookfield and Oliver Griswold write of these subjects with an authority and an authenticity that has long been wanting, and they have done so entertainingly.

Intentionally, they deal with details of natural history only incidentally, presumably reserving extensive treatment of that vast and fascinating phase of the area for the future.

> John D. Pennekamp,
> Associate Editor, The Miami Herald
> Legislative Chairman,
> The Everglades National Park Commission

Acknowledgements

In preparing even such an unpretentious book as this from documents, maps, and widely-scattered old volumes, some of them exceedingly rare, a great deal of help has been needed. The authors wish especially to thank:

The Miami Herald for arrangement to use some of this material which appeared previously as a series in its Sunday editions;

George J. Deedmeyer of Coconut Grove for generous use of many items in his exceptional collection of Floridiana;

For advice in research and use of materials—David O. True; Dr. Charlton W. Tebeau, University of Miami, Editor of Tequesta; Dr. Dorothy Dodd, The Florida State Library; Dr. John C. Gifford, University of Miami; Dr. A. J. Hanna, Rollins College; Senator Spessard L. Holland; Dr. John M. Goggin, University of Florida; and Dr. William C. Sturtevant, Smithsonian Institution;

The National Audubon Society, The National Archives, The Library of Congress, The Key West Library, and The Miami Daily News;

For editing and suggestions, Mrs. Helen Hunter Griswold; for assistance in preparing the manuscript, David M. Walters.

Contents

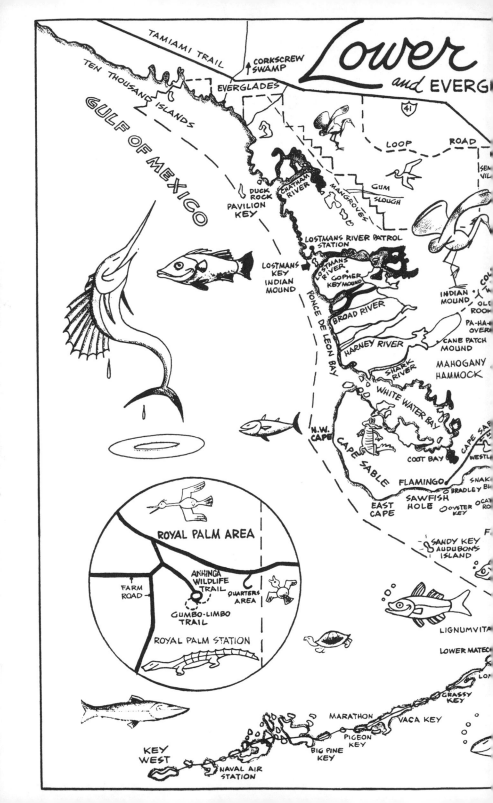

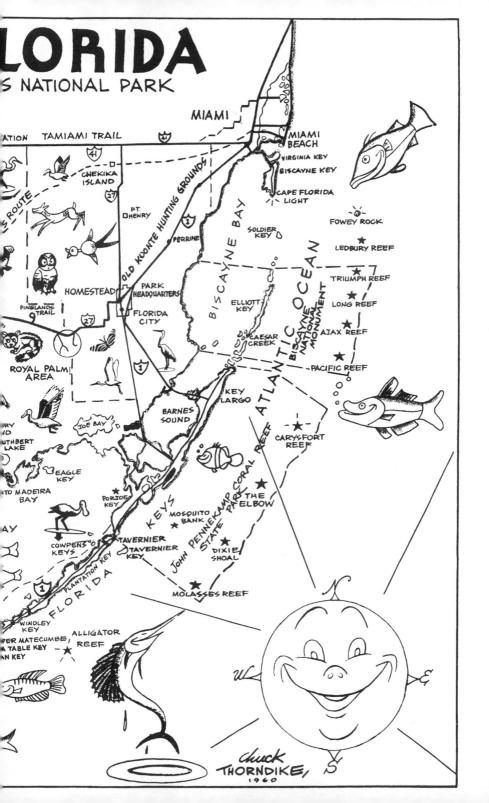

FLORIDA
S NATIONAL PARK

TION   TAMIAMI TRAIL   41   MIAMI

MIAMI
BEACH

VIRGINIA KEY

BISCAYNE KEY

CAPE FLORIDA
LIGHT

FOWEY ROCK

LEDBURY REEF

CHEKIKA
ISLAND   27

PT
D.HENRY

PERRINE   1

SOLDIER
KEY

TRIUMPH REEF

LONG REEF

ROUTE

HOMESTEAD   PARK
HEADQUARTERS

ELLIOTT
KEY

AJAX REEF

PINGLANOS
TRAIL   27

FLORIDA
CITY

CAESAR
CREEK

PACIFIC REEF

ROYAL PALM
AREA   1

BISCAYNE BAY

BISCAYNE OCEAN   NATIONAL MONUMENT

KEY
LARGO

ATLANTIC

BARNES
SOUND

JOE BAY

CARYSFORT
REEF

RY
ND
UTHBERT
LAKE

EAGLE
KEY

TO MADEIRA
BAY

PORTOE
KEY   THE
ELBOW

CORAL REEF

KEYS   MOSQUITO
BANK

John PENNEKAMP STATE PARK

AY

COWPENS
KEYS   TAVERNIER
TAVERNIER
KEY   DIXIE
SHOAL

PLANTATION KEY   1

FLORIDA

MOLASSES REEF

WINDLEY
KEY

PER MATECUMBE
TABLE KEY
AN KEY   ALLIGATOR
REEF

chuck
THORNDIKE,
1960

Sherds from the Cape Sable Shore *Oliver Griswold*

A Caloosa conch shell hoe or pick *Oliver Griswold*

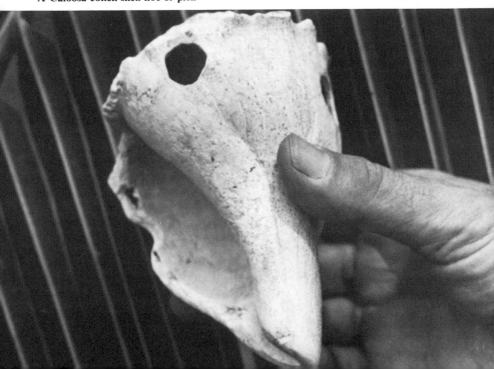

The pine rim of the Everglades

The primival beach at Cape Sable

Oliver Griswold

*Historical Association of
Southern Florida*

The Cape Sable Story

EARLY INDIANS

Always there are voices at lonely Cape Sable.

On this uttermost tip of the Florida mainland, myriad flocks of great birds compose incomparable wilderness music, as they have since the beginning of time.

They have provided the symphonic accompaniment to a great American saga.

When establishment of the Everglades National Park was under discussion, the uninformed said that a bullfrog would knock his brains out trying to get around in this area. It was impenetrable, they said, and empty of human history or meaning.

But the Cape Sable scene and its Everglades surroundings have been the stage for a pageant of colorful people. It holds, today, besides its wealth of unusual wildlife, relics left by the vigorous men who have come and gone. Some left only their bones.

The theme and the mood for this human drama are set by the birds. Their voices are bassoons, trumpets, kettle drums and wailing clarinets, plus sound effects that are unearthly.

Go only a few miles south of Miami to hear it—out on the road beyond Homestead, southwest toward Florida Bay and the Cape. Stop at sunset, when whispering wings of ibises, herons and cormorants make celestial whirrings as they hurry into the mangroves and willows to roost.

Go when the Everglades glow is waning, when the wash of gold and violet fills the sky from zenith to horizon. The birds are most vocal at this hour, just as they were when the Caloosa Indians lived on the shore of Cape Sable between the sparkling sea and the bay that is called Whitewater.

The birds were there then, when the aborigines dug their canal, still visible today, across the neck of the Cape.

They were there when the Spaniards thereabouts got their first look at the continent and when early Americans from Key Largo, Indian Key, Matecumbe and Key West went to the Cape for deer meat and fish and alligator hides and egret plumes.

They were there when a man named Audubon came to paint. They were there when Dr. Henry Perrine planned to build a great agricultural colony and tropical plant introduction station near the

Cape, and when Capt. Jacob Housman offered to kill the warring Indians for $200 a head.

They hovered over the island hammock when Lt. Col. Harney finally hung the bitter chief, Chekika. They were there when Henry Morrison Flagler planned to make the Cape the terminus for his overseas railroad to link Florida with Cuba and South America.

It was for the lacey egret plumes, worth twice their weight in gold, that hunters murdered Audubon Society Warden Guy M. Bradley there. The killing stimulated the development of the National Audubon Society. It energized the dramatic legal fight for Everglades bird protection—first a state, then a national and international victory.

The old schemes and dreams to exploit the Cape Sable area for personal advantage have ended. Turns of destiny have removed its primitive red dwellers. Of its would-be white settlers, all but a few have gone.

Now that it is being used for the enjoyment and enlightenment of the people of the United States, it begins as a national park almost empty of human inhabitants.

But in the previous centuries—first there were many Indians.

The life of the copper-hued dwellers was noted by early observers. A few years before the American revolution, when Florida was British, Capt. Bernard Romans carefully charted the coast and keys of Florida.

His "directions to navigators," compiled from personal explorations in this "difficult part of the world," give clear clues to the aboriginal life of Cape Sable which, in French, means "Sandy Point."

"At Sandy Point, the southern extremity of the peninsula," Romans wrote, "are large old fields, being the land formerly planted by the Caloosa savages."

At nearby Sandy Key, he reported, "are always plenty of flamingoes, plovers and other excellent water fowl to be had. Northwest four miles from this key is Punta Tancha, or Sandy Point; here was anciently a settlement of Caloosa savages. Tolerable water, and excellent venison are to be had here."

Today, fragments of pottery uncovered by waves on wide beaches at the Cape verify Romans' observations. Rim pieces pierced with holes show these ancient people carried their pots with thongs and hung them over cooking fires, where some baked to a sooty black.

A few highly decorated pieces reveal their fondness for ornamentation. Decorations are incised lines forming geometrical patterns about the rim, while hundreds of tiny punctations within the motif serve to emphasize the design. From these potsherds, archeologists estimate these people lived on the Cape for nearly two thousand years.

14

To learn more specifically about the primitive inhabitants, we go back four hundred years—to the days when streams of gold and silver from the New World were flowing, like a transfusion, into the veins of old Spain, giving her strength to become, for two centuries, the most powerful nation on earth.

It was customary for wealthy families in the Spanish New World to ship their youngsters to the mother country for schooling. Thirteen-year-old Hernando d'Escalente Fontaneda, en route to Spain, was shipwrecked on the Florida Keys. For 17 years he was a captive of the Indians.

Finally rescued from this slavery, he was taken to Spain. He wrote a "Memoir," a detailed description of what he had seen, of "the things, the shore and the Indians of Florida."

"In the territory of Carlos, a province of Indians, which in their language signifies a fierce people, they are so called for being brave and skillful, as in truth they are," Fontaneda wrote. "They are masters of a large district of country, as far as a town they call Guacata, on the Lake of Mayaimi, which is called Mayaimi because it is very large."

Mayaimi became Maymi, then Miami. The name was given first to the river, then to the town. Lake Mayaimi of the Caloosas was later called by the Seminoles, "Okeechobee," which also means "big water."

Carlos was sometimes spelled Callos. But into fairly modern times it was used in Carloosahatchie, meaning River of Carlos, now spelled Caloosahatchie.

The land of Carlos, according to Fontaneda, extended from a large town in the north on the West Coast, called "Tampa," southward to the lower Florida Keys, and up the East Coast to "Quisiyove," probably on Hobe Sound. There were fifty or more towns and many villages. Most were on the coast where seafood was plentiful. The coastal town, "Casitoa," may have been the one on Cape Sable.

The Cape, with its wealth of wildlife, could easily support a numerous population. Great numbers of turtles struggled up on the sand to lay hundreds of eggs. Quaintly, the raccoon, which was unknown in Spain, was described as "a certain animal that looks like a fox, yet is not, but a different thing from it. It is fat and good to eat."

Large bears were killed, also "sea wolves." Later explorers saw seals on the Florida Reef, although "sea wolves" to some of them might have been manatee. Ponce de Leon recorded killing 14 "sea wolves" in the Dry Tortugas.

These animals, however, were evidently scarce, for it was reported that only the upper class Indians, who had first choice, enjoyed such delicacies.

In Capt. Romans' time, vessels needing food sent hunters to the Cape for the plentiful game. He wrote: "I was once in great want of provisions at Matacombe and sent a hunter with a boy in a

15

skiff to the westward, at Sandy Point or Cape Sable; whence he returned in a few days, with 13 large and very fat deer, properly salted and cured, which were excellent provisions for us for several days."

Edible wild fruits of species now found in the Cape area probably provided much food for the Caloosas—cocoplums, pigeon plums, the heart and berries of the cabbage palm, the royal palm, the wild papaya and many others. Centuries later, the great pioneer in American plant introduction, Dr. Perrine, chose this site for his experiments because it was so naturally verdant.

It is not surprising that the people of Carlos lived well and became the dominant power in South Florida. From conch shells, they made dippers and cups, hoes, picks and tomahawks, possibly the origin of our slang expression, "conched on the dome."

What was cultivated in the "large old fields" of the early Caloosas? No remains of the vegetables, of course, have been preserved in the mounds of earth, bone and shell that rise on the most ancient Indian town sites. Could it be that the Opuntia, or prickly pear, now found on the Cape, are descendants of those grown by the primitive Indians?

Gray Florida moss, really an air-plant, was used by the Caloosa women to make neat skirts. It is frequently found on trees near old Indian mounds on the Keys, many miles from its usual habitat.

Caloosa men, clean-limbed and strong, wore breech cloths of woven palm fiber or of deer skin. The useful thatch palm still grows on the Cape. Deer are scarce today, but should again be plentiful in the sanctuary of the Everglades National Park.

For hunting and war, the Caloosas used the bow and arrow and spears hurled from a crotched stick. With these weapons, under Chief Carlos, they fiercely withstood repeated incursions of the Spaniards and dealt the famed Ponce de Leon his death wound. All South Florida tribes paid the Caloosas tribute.

Like the whites of today, they built canals, although not for the doubtful value of drainage, but for short-cuts by canoe. Not far east of Cape Sable, the present road crosses an ancient Indian canal connecting Mud Lake and Florida Bay. Through this, the canoes could safely pass inland to the west coast, avoiding the rough waters around the Cape.

Near the Mud Lake end of this now overgrown and silted channel stand earth mounds, full of charred remains of centuries-old cooking fires, and the bones of animals, alligators and turtles.

Nearby once grew stately Florida royal palms, named Roystonea by botanists for General Roy Stone of the U. S. Army. The palms furnished food for the early people. The hurricane of 1935 blew out the tops and growing buds of all but one tree. Now the dead, gray trunks rise like graveyard monuments to the memory of the first inhabitants.

The Caloosas were numbered in the thousands, when the Spanish slave hunters and adventurers came. But the Caloosa nation dwindled under the attacks of Creek Indians, their stronger enemies to the north, who came by way of the St. Johns River, took them captive and sold them as slaves.

The remaining Caloosas took refuge in the intricate Ten Thousand Islands and southward in the remote island bays and labyrinths of the Shark River. On the banks of the Harney, the Broad and the Shark Rivers, Capt. Romans reported, "we meet with some hills of rich soil and on every one of those the evident marks of their having been formerly cultivated by the savages. These hills . . . have apparently been the last retreats and skulking places of the Caloosa savages."

About 80 families, supposedly the last remnant of this once-powerful tribe, were driven down into the Florida Keys. They became known as Spanish Indians. On the surface, they were friendly to the Spaniards and learned their tongue; but they brutally murdered shipwrecked mariners of other nationalities.

When the English occupied Florida in 1763, these 80 families evacuated to Havana, fearing retaliation for their brutality to British sailors. But this was not the last of all the Spanish Indians, for no white man then knew who or what was in the heart of the mysterious Everglades.

Some of them long afterward inhabited the lower Everglades. Joined by Seminoles and fugitive slaves, and stealthily supplied by American-hating Spaniards, they were the terror of the Second Seminole War. Many were killed. Some were captured and transported to a western reservation.

As late as 1903, however, Dr. John C. Gifford, professor of tropical forestry at the University of Miami, visited a remote island hammock in the Everglades. Here he found a small village of "different" Indians cultivating the dasheen, sweet potato, and hard-skinned Okeechobee squash. Dr. Gifford described them as definitely unlike the Seminoles in dress and physical appearance.

These may have been the last of the Caloosas.

Many a Brave Ship

Ponce de Leon called them "Los Martires."

He said the coral reefs off the Florida Keys that curve in a protecting arc around Cape Sable looked like agonized men skewered on stakes in martyrdom.

From Ponce's time on, as the Martyrs, the reefs have been the terror of navigators. Many a brave ship, helpless in stormy seas, has been impaled.

Galleons laden with treasure, rich merchantmen, proud ships of the line, and even modern steamers, have strewed their precious cargoes and hulls along the Martyrs. Notably, fleets bound for Old Spain, heavy with gold and silver plate and coin from Mexico and Peru, crashed to destruction.

The cannon and coin of old wrecks are still being found today. Along the keys and at the Cape, treasure hunters with electronic metal-detectors, hew hopefully through the jungle or dive into the depths off shore—sometimes with results.

In the 17th century three ships of the line were dispatched by the British to harry the French in the West Indies. Loaded with loot, but with disease daily decimating the officers and crews, they returned through the Florida Straits. In September 1695, one of them, the 60-gun H.M.S. Winchester, struck the Martyrs and sank.

Not until 1940 did a party of Miamians discover and raise guns, coins and silver plate. Preserved by the 245-year-old crust of coral were even fragments of a prayer book, with the Litany of Loreto still readable in Latin.

If the exact location of the ill-fated ship had not remained unknown until 1940, there might be a "Winchester Reef" on the charts today.

Many a ledge on the Florida Reef bears the name of a ship wrecked or stranded there long ago. Some, like the Fowey, for which dangerous rocks are now named, were British war vessels christened for English towns. The Ledbury, for example, a kind of brig known as a "snow," was driven ashore in the great hurricane of 1769. Originally, a nearby island was named for her. Later it was changed to Elliott Key; but Ledbury Reef, northeast of the key, still commemorates her loss.

His Majesty's frigate Carysfort left her bones in 1770 on the reef now known by her name.

The first salvagers, or wreckers, were the Indians of the keys and the southern tip of the mainland. From the wrecks that began piling on the shores soon after the white men came to the New World, the natives quickly learned the value of money and the delights of being so freely furnished with all manner of useful goods.

At first, they slaughtered or enslaved shipwrecked mariners of every nation. Each sailor or passenger who escaped the cruel sea fell victim ashore to a death more horrible.

But as the power of Spain grew, the Indians, either because of fear or friendship, limited their depredations to vessels and men of other countries. As skilled divers and boatmen, they were often employed by the Spaniards to salvage treasure.

The English never lost a chance to hi-jack the Spanish wealth that had been filched originally from Aztecs or Incas. In 1716, a British ship carried word to Jamaica that in passing the Martyrs it had seen Spaniards raising the treasure from a fleet of galleons wrecked there two years before.

This golden news, the Jamaicans quickly seized. Two ships and four sloops were dispatched under Capt. Henry Jennings. From small boats the Spaniards and Indians were diving up the metal.

Brought ashore to Key Largo, the treasures were guarded by a company of soldiers. When the Jamaican fleet hove into sight, the Spaniards hustled coins and plate into every conceivable cranny. They stuffed it away until they were forced to flee for their lives.

Capt. Jennings recovered 350,000 pieces of eight. How many did he miss? Some, at any rate. Caches that Jennings missed have been found in modern times.

Responsibility for the loss of several large Spanish plate fleets rests with vain admirals, who in some instances must have been political appointees with little knowledge of the sea. Such was Admiral Don Roderigo de Torres, commanding 14 galleons returning to Old Spain with a great treasure in the year 1733.

One of his captains, an old sea dog who knew danger when he saw it, risked his neck by disobeying the pompous admiral's signals, but saved his ship. All thirteen others rammed on the Martyrs east of Key Largo. For years, Indians and Spaniards dived up the gold and silver.

But not all of the cargoes lost along the Martyrs were claimed by the reefs themselves. For centuries, the Spanish ships suffered from English, French and Dutch buccaneers. By 1819, however, the picture was reversed. Spanish pirates based mainly in Cuba, but also using the Florida Keys for rendezvous, preyed on all other nations, particularly the United States.

By then, some of Spain's colonies had begun a struggle for independence. Spain declared blockade of their ports. The colonies, in turn, declared blockade of all ports still loyal to Spain. They were lush days for piracy. Under pretext of enforcing one blockade or another, the free-booters boarded hundreds of ships.

Crews and passengers were brutally tortured to force them to tell the hiding place of valuables. When empty of information they were hacked to death, burned or drowned.

Decrepit Spain could not cope with the estimated 10,000 blood-thirsty thieves infesting the Cuban coasts and the Florida Straits. Corrupt Spanish officials winked at merchants who purchased the pirates' spoils. Cargoes were plundered even in the harbors of Matanzas and Havana.

One reason the United States wanted Florida from Spain in 1819 was to suppress the bloody butchers. Their boldness in robbing the trade around the tip of Florida was incredible and was a drag on development of the Louisiana Purchase through the port of New Orleans.

Spurred by the clamoring American public and press, Congress appropriated for an expedition to rout the raiders. Command was given to an able and determined veteran, Commodore David Porter. Soon after Florida became U. S. territory, he based at Key West (then called Thompson's Island after the Secretary of the Navy) and ran the pirates ragged.

Most famous of his ships was the schooner U.S.S. Alligator. Under Lieut. W. H. Allen, the Alligator pursued a fleet of eight pirate vessels in November 1822. The wind was light. Allen's 40 men took to their small boats and oars to overhaul them. The pirates totalled 125 men and had 14 cannon. Allen's party had muskets, swords and pistols.

In the bloody hand-to-hand fighting, five pirate ships were taken. But Allen, wounded twice, died before final victory. "Allen" became the Navy war cry in many later battles. Key West was one time named Allenton.

Only a few days after Allen's death, the Martyrs claimed his proud schooner. Alligator Light, a powerful beam shining afar from a steel structure above the reef of that name now warns ships of the dangerous ledge.

Possibly the last ship actually plundered in the Florida Keys was the Emma Sophia bound from Hamburg to Havana. Just a year before Florida became a part of the U. S., the Emma Sophia was proceeding peacefully through the Santaren Channel between Cuba and the Great Bahama Bank.

She was taken to "a small port between the Florida Isles and the Martyrs Reef." Vessel and crew were there stripped of everything valuable by a band of pirates captained by a Spaniard flying "the blood-red flag."

Because few witnesses of actual pirate boardings survived, first-hand accounts of their butchery are rare. Torture was applied first to ships' officers to wring the secret locations of money and valuables. Having witnessed these crimes, the passengers and crew were next eliminated.

TMS Winchester guns had been sunk for 245 years

Coins from wrecks on the Florida Reef

John James Audubon

Port of Key West in 1838

White Pelican by Audubon

Roseate Spoonbill by Audubon

Historical Association of Southern Florida

Tales of the few, who through some quirk escaped, surpass the most fiendish imagination. One captain, for instance, to make him reveal hidden money, was first slowly lacerated repeatedly with a cutlass. When he still wouldn't talk, first one arm, then the other, was chopped off at the elbow.

After he managed to shriek out the information, the pirates soaked a pile of oakum with turpentine. They stuffed a big wad between his teeth, lighted it, and threw him into the oakum pile. From the torch in his mouth, the heap quickly flamed up and roasted him.

Most of the marauding wretches blew their blood-soaked booty drinking and carousing in the towns of Cuba. But sometimes they buried it, intending to retrieve it later. Over the years and recently the Florida Keys and the mainland tip have rewarded searchers. Sometimes it has been several hundred pounds of gold and silver coins in a pitch-sealed hole in the rocks. Sometimes a hefty clay jar of gold religious medals originally snatched from the necks of many victims, or a helmet of silver or a pot of doubloons have come to light; but more often just a piece of corroded jewelry.

Only cannon or huge anchors remain to mark the graves of treasure-bearing wrecks still below the waters. Unless the hulls lie in deep, cold water, sea worms have destroyed all wood. Stories of coral-encrusted galleon hulls seen from the surface should be discounted. No one knows or can ever calculate the tedious hours and days that have been devoted to treasure hunts. It still goes on.

As this article was being written, this cryptic message came in the mail:

"Dear mister charles we found what you leave us to look for. too one place in 16 feet water. we try them. white courles. i strik them no russ no were. they muss be brass we lik to see you."

This means an island friend has found the last resting place of an ancient vessel. In 16 feet of water he has found two cannon in an area of white coral. Since, when he struck them, there was no rust anywhere, they must be of brass.

Examination of the gun-maker's marks on them will reveal their nationality, approximate age, and, maybe, the ship's identity. Perhaps it was a treasure ship manned by men who, like Ponce de Leon, called the Florida Reef "Los Martires."

Wreckers to the Rescue

The cumbersome Spanish treasure ships, en route from Mexico to Spain, sailed safely down the west shore of Florida. Only on the east coast they crashed—often.

Why? The answer comes colorfully from an early and now exceedingly rare English history.

"The galleons in their passage from Vera Cruz to Havana," William Roberts explained, "are obliged by reason of the Northeast Trade Winds to stretch away northward. As soon as they have made La Sunda, they keep as near the coast of Florida as possible and generally fall in with some men-of-war to convoy them to Havana."

La Sunda was the old Spanish name for the long banks running out from Florida's west coast. Shoaling up gradually from navigable depths to shoreline, they gave ample warning of the land's proximity. If westerly winds threatened to press the ships too close in shore, the banks afforded firm anchorage.

On fair, offshore winds, then, the galleons coasted south by the Indian towns that flourished there even as late as 1750, past the Ten Thousand Islands, and the mouths of many rivers draining the Everglades.

From the high poops of the lumbering vessels, the anxious captains could mark the great mangroves of Shark River, that like an army of giants marched toward them into the sea. The same towering forest is there today to amaze visitors to the Everglades National Park. Some botanists believe they may be the parent mangrove forest of the world.

A few miles southward, the galleons passed tall palm clusters on the shining beaches of Cape Sable.

They used them for point of departure for the Dry Tortugas Islands. Beyond lay the haven of Havana.

The next leg of the course for the treasure fleets that rendezvoused in Havana was beset with danger. Like the ancient Greeks who had to pass between Scylla and Charybdis, the galleons had the Great Bahama Bank on one hand, and on the other, the fearsome Florida Reef.

Here the sounding leads gave but short warning of perils. The coral ledges rose sheer from the deep. When the danger was discovered, and the vessels frantically dropped anchor to windward, it was usually too late. In the great depths and on the hard bottom, the hooks rarely took hold in time.

26

Beginning with the galleons, and for centuries after, the coral teeth of the Florida Reef tore out the vitals of ships carelessly navigated or helplessly battered before raging hurricanes.

When the British took over Florida from the Spanish, the Indians of the keys—fearing retribution for the inhuman treatment they had given British sailors cast away on the reefs—soon left in a body for Havana. With the savages gone, the way was now clear for Bahama turtlers and wood-cutters to take over the wrecking. The Bahamans, or "Conchs," anchored their sailing craft in summer off Key Tabona (now Tavernier) to wait for ships returning from Jamaica to England on the summer winds.

Enough ships failed to steer clear of the reefs to make a good business for the "Conchs," who first assisted the shipwrecked people, then salvaged the cargoes. They took them to Bahaman or Cuban ports.

As commerce developed between ports of the Gulf and the outside seas, the reef's hungry maw claimed more and more. Soon after the U. S. bought Florida, the communities of Key West and Indian Key sprang into existence as wrecking stations.

Rich cargoes of raw materials for the North and for Europe included baled cotton and rice from the Louisiana Purchase and pine from Pensacola. From Mexico came cochineal, logwood, hides and sisal. In the return trade, made-goods—brocades and silverware, wines and carriages, textiles and shoes—fell into the hands of the wreckers.

Everything that the commerce of the world afforded reached Key West as salvage. As early as 1824, a year's worth of wrecked goods landed at the embryo port brought $293,000—all big, old-fashioned dollars that required only a few to make a man rich. The government collected more than $100,000 in import duties.

By 1835, there were 20 sizeable vessels engaged in wrecking, hailing from New York and such Connecticut ports as Mystic and Groton, as well as Key West, Key Vacas and Indian Key. Many of the Cockney-speaking "Conchs" from the Bahamas came to man some of the ships with the "Downeasters" or work as laborers, clerks or proprietors in the warehouses.

The peak came in the decade 1850-60. Five hundred wrecks, or nearly one a week, hit the reefs. The value of just the ships was over $16,000,000. Wrecking was big business. Fleets of fast schooners and sloops, manned by seamen whose courage and ability were unsurpassed, were employed by large companies.

Their trim vessels, assigned to sections, patrolled the 200 mile arc of coral from Key Biscayne to the Dry Tortugas. Their first function was to save lives. There was no U. S. Coast Guard then.

Next, they tried to save the ship, and many were refloated, brought in, and repaired. But if the ship had rammed on too hard and ripped her hull and bilged beyond recovery, as was often the case, then all hands worked to salvage the cargo.

The wreckers were paid off in shares, adjudicated in the early days by juries, but later by superior court.

Many a modern South Florida name is descended from survivors who first stepped on these shores from the decks of rescuing wrecking vessels—such names as Browne, Filer, Wall, Thompson, Whitehead, Knight, Reynolds and Lester.

Feeble, indeed, were the early efforts of the government to warn mariners of the reefs. By 1850, only two aids to navigation had been placed, a lighthouse on Cape Florida, and inside Carysfort Reef a lightship which was seldom on exact station.

Both were attacked during the Seminole Wars. The lighthouse was burned out. Frequently storms blew the lightship off station. Mariners placed little confidence in it.

As early as 1835, the Key West Enquirer editorialized on government neglect, since "from Carysfort to Key West, a distance of 120 miles, there is no light."

Despite the facts of "no light," romantic tales of false lights to lure vessels to destruction are still told along the Keys today. Apparently these were inspired by the lore of old England brought by the Bahama settlers. The stories date back at least two hundred years, for even in those early times, Capt. Romans recounted:

"And as for the idle tales of their making false lights along the shores, I can from many years experience assure it to be an untruth. Those fires are occasioned by the hunters and timber cutters, who burn the woods to clear them of the under-wood, and to procure fresh pasture for the deer. Lightning also often sets fire to trees; and I have frequently in very dry seasons seen spontaneous fires arise in marshy places.

"But after all, what business has a mariner (who knows the course he must steer) to follow any light out of that course? And I would just hint to everyone who passes along this coast that on seeing a light to the westward, it behooves him to look out for breakers if he stands in for that quarter."

It was 1852, in fact, before the lightship at Carysfort was replaced by the present 110-foot lighthouse, the first of the chain of tall beacons completed by the turn of the century to warn of dangers from Fowey Rocks off Miami to Loggerhead Key in the Dry Tortugas.

With these aids to safety, the terrors of the reef diminished. The ecstatic cry of "Wreck Ashore!" that rang so frequently through the streets of Key West gradually died away.

Although steam replaced sail, human ingenuity, however, could not entirely overcome human frailty, or the overwhelming forces of the sea at its worst—the unpredicted hurricane.

Old-timers still tell of rich cargoes salvaged from great steamers grounded through errors in navigation. The unexpected velocity of the Gulf Stream played tricks with mariners' taffrail logs, giving wrong speed data. Distances were miscalculated. Misplotted courses brought catastrophe to the ships—joy to the wreckers.

The Spanish steamer Alicia, out of Bilbao for Havana in 1905, took bottom 30 miles from Miami on a reef already named for the Ajax, wrecked there three-quarters of a century before.

After great labor by highly-organized modern wrecking equipment, the Alicia was got off. But a sudden squall piled her on again —this time to stay.

Soon a polyglot fleet of sailing craft swarmed around to take the salvage from her holds. Although bilged and much of her freight water-logged, there was much more to save. Two crews of 50 men each braced themselves on her canted decks and heaved in unison on the great unloading tackles.

Sensing the values of the boxes and bales they swung over the sides, their voices rolled out over the water as they lifted old sea chanties in throaty rhythm to time their lusty team-work. Excitedly, they eyed each load as it rose above decks, appraised every bulging item as the cargo nets poised over the schooners, and laughed joyously in anticipation of their shares.

It was wrecking as of the days of old, the match for any tale of their forebears on the reef.

Linens and laces, silks and satins, household goods and provisions, pianos, wines and furniture came out of the Alicia's holds. That night a cask of wine, thrown over the side, was towed to Captain Lowe's beach on Elliott Key. Cups were hung on a ring of nails driven around the cask, the bung was started, and the jolly wreckers danced for joy in the moonlight.

Capt. Lowe salvaged several grand pianos. His house was so stuffed with goods that he slept in the kitchen and cooked in the woodshed. Folks on the Keys appeared at Sunday service in remarkable finery.

The Alicia is remembered as the last of the "good" wrecks. A chunk of her hull still juts above the surface of the battering waves on Ajax Reef, last reminder of days of tragedy, salvage profits and derring-do.

The U. S. Coast Guard has now taken over the saving of lives and ships, and the colorful career of the old-time wrecker has come to an end.

Ornithologist With a Paint Brush

The two most colorful men concerned with birds in the Everglades National Park area were a painter of world renown and a little known game warden.

The ornithologist and bird painter, John James Audubon, made his explorations there in 1832. Still a vital influence in popular American natural history, Audubon's accounts of his trip stand vividly today as delightful contributions to the history of the area.

Guy M. Bradley, the warden, likely had more to do with changing the styles in women's hats than any other Floridian. He died in the name of Audubon, an employee of the National Audubon Society, while protecting the egrets from commercial hunters supplying the millinery trade.

Bradley is buried under a marker placed by the Florida (State) Audubon Society at Cape Sable. His murder in 1905 by a plume hunter crystallized and energized the conservation program of the National Society that eventually saved the birds—and forced the bonnet trade to give up "aigrettes."

Between Audubon's visit and Bradley's fight to save the birds, nearly three-quarters of a century intervened. So the Audubon tale comes first.

His fame had already been achieved substantially when he landed on the Florida Keys. The first of his great series, "Birds of America," had been published. He had letters from the Secretaries of Navy and of Treasury directing the captains of vessels of war and of revenue cutters to transport him about.

His own records discredit the oft-repeated statement that he was disappointed in Florida. He made bitter remarks. But they were about the St. Augustine and St. John's River country.

On the Florida Keys he had a wonderful time. Lavishly he praised the people and the riches of bird life.

He found new birds, one entirely new to science, several new to him, and one species that has never been seen since in North America. If he had stayed a bit longer at Cape Sable, he might have added another "first." He missed the Cape Sable seaside sparrow, which was not discovered in its exclusive strip of habitat for nearly 100 years.

This blithe little hopper, once frequently seen there, looks very much like the tourists who come to see him. His markings make him look for all the world as if he were wearing the current vogue in sun-glasses.

Audubon made a hit in Key West. The Geiger house, still standing today, is pointed out as a place where he was entertained ashore. The little newspaper published in 1832 on that already bustling island reported that Audubon visited there May 4, the "fifty-second anniversary of his birth."

The comment is significant. Audubon's birth date and place have been much argued. He added to the confusion himself by sometimes giving one, sometimes another, for he enjoyed keeping alive the suspicion that he was really the Dauphin of France who had mysteriously disappeared during the French Revolution.

But whether he was 52 years old or 47, when he was in Key West, did not disturb the editor's forthright appraisal.

"This gentleman left here on the revenue cutter Marion on Monday last for Charleston," the article reported, "calculating to touch on his way at the Florida Keys and probably the mainland.

"It affords us great pleasure to state that his expedition has given him much satisfaction and added largely to his collection of specimens, etc.

"Mr. Audubon is a most extraordinary man, possessed of an ardent and enthusiastic mind and entirely devoted to his pursuits; danger cannot daunt, and difficulties vanish before him.

"During his stay here, his hour of rising was three o'clock in the morning; from then until noon and sometimes even until night, he was engaged in hunting among the mangrove keys, despite of heat, sand-flies and mosquitoes.

"On his return from these expeditions, his time was principally employed in making sketches of such plants and birds as he may have procured. This was not the extraordinary effort for a day. It was continued for weeks.

"In short, it appeared to constitute his chief aim, as it is his happiness. Mr. Audubon has adopted a most excellent plan of connecting with his drawings of birds such plants as may be found in the neighborhood where they are taken. We hesitate not in giving it as our opinion that his works on ornithology, when completed, will be the most splendid production of its kind ever published, and we trust that it will be duly estimated and patronized.

"The private character of Mr. Audubon corresponds with the nature of his mind and pursuits—he is frank, free and generous, always willing to impart information, and to render himself agreeable. The favorable impression which he has produced upon our minds will not soon be effaced."

Understandably, the Key West historian, Jefferson B. Browne, erred in stating that Audubon was the first ornithologist to find the beautiful white-crowned pigeon in the United States. The slip is worth noting, not so much as a criticism of Browne, who made no claim as a bird specialist, but because his innocently-made statement has often been cribbed and widely spread by unknowing writers.

Audubon, 'tis true, did use a local specimen for his famed painting of the snowy-topped, purplish migrant from Cuba and the West Indies that still comes to nest on the keys and the mainland tip in spring and summer. But the species was already known.

Titian R. Peale, artist and naturalist employed by Charles Lucien Bonaparte, had found it in 1824.

For his great rendezvous with South Florida bird life, Audubon was rowed some 20 miles from Indian Key off the Matecumbes, across the Bay of Florida, to Sandy Key. This L-shaped island lies about six miles off Cape Sable.

It was an extremely heavily-populated rookery in 1832. When Audubon laid down on the sand to sleep the first night, the waters almost touched his feet. When he opened his eyes in the morning, the tide had retreated to an immense distance, exposing vast flats. His boat lay out of water on her side, looking like a whale reposing on a mud bank.

The birds in myriads were probing their wet pasture ground. He saw great flocks of ibises feeding apart from equally large collections of godwits. Thousands of herons gracefully paced the soft surface, thrusting their javelin bills into fish in the small pools.

"Frigate pelicans," Audubon wrote, "chased the jaeger, which himself had just robbed a poor gull of its prize; and all the gallinules ran with spread wings from the mud banks to the thickets of the island, so timorous had they become when they perceived us."

The frigate pelicans are now called man-o'-war birds.

Audubon and his aides dared not venture out on the treacherous mud. His guide assured him that nothing would be lost by waiting. After a breakfast of ibis eggs that had been found in every bush, the party prepared to collect birds.

"Over these flats, a foot or two of water is quite sufficient to drive all the birds ashore, even the tallest heron or flamingo," Audubon observed.

Each of his party, provided with a gun, posted himself behind a bush. Immediately the tide forced the waders to shore, the shooting commenced.

"When it at length ceased," Audubon wrote, "the collected mass of birds of different kinds looked not unlike a small haycock. Who could not with a little industry have helped himself to a few of these skins? Why, reader, no one so fond of these things as I am. Every one assisted in this, and even the sailors themselves tried their hand at the work."

In modern times, such killing would seem wanton. But Audubon did not permit killing beyond what was needed for proper specimens for his paintings—and to feed his expedition. To have examples of correct plumage of mature birds, and to prevent the error of portraying an immaturely-feathered one for an adult, he had to study many skins in hand. Even with all his care in observation and collecting, he made such a mistake in one of his notable paintings.

In those days, too, without refrigeration and other modern camping supplies, it was largely necessary to live on the land.

Among the specimens of that day's collecting, Audubon discovered the great white heron—the bird that appears on the Everglades National Park postage stamp. He named it *Ardea occidentalis*.

The largest of American herons, on seven-foot wing spread it ponderously beats out its floating, gliding flight across the mangroves. Why hadn't it been identified by scientists before? Probably because even within its restricted habitat it wasn't as common as the many other huge birds, and nobody had been that way with observation as keen as Audubon's.

Perhaps, too, it had been mistaken for the American egret, with which it is still often confused, although the egret is somewhat smaller and has black legs, instead of yellow.

Among Audubon's specimens of that trip were three that have made unique ornithological history. A trio of European greenshanks he collected there were the only ones that have ever been seen in the United States, even to this day. One of the skins is believed to be still in the National Museum in Washington.

Another rarity he collected was the Key West quail-dove, known only from that island. Only a few have been seen after Audubon's time, and none in recent years. Likewise, the zenaida dove he observed seems to have disappeared from the keys.

Whether Audubon himself actually set foot on the mainland tip is a nice question. He said only, "Having filled our cask from a fine well, long since dug in the sand of Cape Sable, either by Seminole Indians or pirates, no matter which, we left Sandy Isle about full tide, and proceeded homewards, giving a call here and there at different keys with the view of procuring rare birds, and also their nests and eggs."

Returning to Indian Key, Audubon experienced a hurricane. It was small, but fortunately sprightly enough to inspire him to pen a description that remains a classic in Florida meteorology.

Strangely, a little over a century later, the hurricane of 1935 stripped Sandy Key of its larger trees, so that it has not yet recovered as a great rookery. As a sanctuary, the Audubon Society guarded its recovery until the U. S. Fish and Wildlife Service took over and finally the National Park Service.

Now, under nature's gradual restoration of the island, the Service hopes it will again teem with great birds to thrill modern visitors as the primeval scene thrilled Audubon.

The Blood-Red Years

The maps of Southern Florida for more than a century now have carried the names of four strangely-linked men—Chekika, the Indian; Harney, the soldier; Perrine, the visionary; and Poinsett, the statesman.

The historic places bearing their names are miles apart. Their lives, however, were closely interwoven.

Even a quick glance at the map reveals that the story of the Everglades National Park area could not be told without them. But it takes more than a glance to discover their bizarre connection.

A mile and a quarter south of the Tamiami Trail at approximately 20 miles west of the 1957 Miami city limits, is an Everglades hammock, Chekika's Island.

There, Lt. Col. William S. Harney hanged the body of Chekika. It had already been shot dead by one Private Hall under Harney's command.

South from Miami on the Dixie Highway is the village of Perrine, named for Dr. Henry Perrine, who was killed at Indian Key in 1840 by Chekika's band.

Just north of Cape Sable is the Harney River, navigated by him on his expedition that got Chekika.

Down on the Cape, itself, is the site of old Ft. Poinsett, named for Joel R. Poinsett, Secretary of War in the blood-red years of the Second Seminole war.

Both Poinsett and Harney were involved directly, not only in the dramatic, violent death of Chekika, but also in the cremation of the great Dr. Perrine.

'Tis a tale surpassing fiction. Without the proof of documents, it would be incredible.

Cape Sable was the center of the action sometimes. At others, it was only on the perimeter. But the final fight to make all Florida safe at last for white settlers pivoted largely around Dr. Perrine's scheme to build, near the Cape, a great colony and a scientific plantation for the introduction of tropical plants to enhance the agriculture of the whole United States.

His project was national in scope, designed to carry out high international and internal government policy, and so recognized in the executive and legislative branches in Washington.

Poinsett, he who brought from Mexico the blood-red flower that as the poinsettia perpetuates his name, was one-time United States Minister to Mexico. Perrine, in the same years, was American Consul at the port of Campeche in the Mexican state of Yucatan.

There, the doctor formed his vision of bringing to South Florida a selection of many tropical plants. He would make the peninsula tip rich with crops of fruit, hemp and medicinal plants. They would be developed, acclimatized and then spread throughout the South and the Southwest and beyond.

Poinsett, his superior, approved the plan, as did so many others in high authority. While Perrine was perfecting his Mexican botanical research, Poinsett became Secretary of War.

In Washington, their ways crossed again. The doctor came in 1838 to argue for, and get, his township of Florida land from Congress. He wanted his 24,000 acres to be on the mainland. Although Poinsett still agreed that the project would likely reshape the whole course of American agriculture, he had to say, "No, not for a while."

It was under his direction that the shamefully-prolonged war with the Indians was dragging on.

The previously-quiet South Florida savages were wildly rampant again. White settlers along the lower East Coast, from the New River down, had fled to the Florida Keys. Some had not stopped until they reached Key West.

On the keys, they were considered safe. An amphibious foray across the Bay of Florida was believed beyond the abilities of savages in war canoes. Then, too, there were the protecting troops stationed at Cape Florida on Key Biscayne. A sizable Naval force protected the county seat of Dade County at Indian Key.

Besides, most of the inhabitants on Key Largo and of the settlement on Key Vacas were salvagers of shipwrecks. Well-equipped with swift sloops and schooners, they could evacuate the entire population at the first hint of a redskin attack.

Down at Key West, an organized armed guard of citizens patrolled the beaches nightly. For a time, the great Frigate Constitution—"Old Ironsides" herself—lay in the harbor with bristling guns.

The southern mainland was in possession of the Indians by virtue of their bloody sallies from the Everglades fastnesses. At will, they popped out, ripped off scalps, garnered up supplies, burned cabins—and once the Cape Florida lighthouse—and disappeared.

So, it was on Indian Key that Dr. Perrine and his family landed.

Major Gen. Thomas S. Jesup, commanding the Florida forces in 1838, pleaded with the War Department for a realistic Indian policy. In a confidential letter he wrote:

"We have committed the error of attempting to remove them when their lands were not required for agricultural purposes; when they were not in the way of white inhabitants, and when the greater portion of their country was an unexplored wilderness, of the interior of which we were as ignorant as of the interior of China."

The general said the nation was employing an army, for the first time since the commencement of history, simply to explore a country and to try to remove savages just from one wilderness to another. He pleaded that the policy of trying to export the Seminoles to Arkansas be given up. He suggested, instead, assigning a Florida reservation and allowing them to remain.

The War Department bluntly replied to get busy and ship the savages to Arkansas.

By then, Perrine had received approval of his ambitious agricultural colony on the mainland. It was a symbol of the objectives for which the white man's civilization pressed on to take over and settle South Florida.

Finally the War Department adopted, in part, Gen. Jesup's view. Major General Alexander Macomb, commander of the whole United States Army, came to Florida to lend weight to negotiations.

He worked through a lieutenant colonel who had previously distinguished himself in the reformation of a delinquent Louisiana character named La Fitte. Recently he had also shown marked ability in handling the Indians. This picked man—Lt. Col. William S. Harney—was told to round up the Indian chiefs from the wilderness below the Miami River and the vicinity of Cape Sable and fetch them to a conference at Ft. King (Ocala).

Gen. Macomb apparently had the right man. In fact, it is possible that the idea of a reservation in Florida for the Indians was originally Harney's.

One of the best appraisals of Harney was written by Jefferson Davis. When Davis was Secretary of War of the United States he knew Harney well.

"He was physically the finest specimen of man I ever saw," Davis wrote. "Tall, straight, muscular, broad-chested, and gaunt-waisted, he was one of the class which Trelawney describes as 'nature's noblemen'. . . .

"Had he lived in the time of Homer, he would have robbed Achilles of his sobriquet of the 'swift-footed,' for he could run faster than a white man, farther than an Indian. . . .

"Harney was also a bold horseman, fond of the chase, a good boatman, and skillful in the use of the spear as a fisherman. Neither drinking nor gaming, he was clear of those rocks and shoals of life in a frontier garrison. . . .

"He had acquired that knowledge of Indian character which was often conspicuously exhibited in his military career."

On his way around from Cape Florida to the West Coast, en route to the Ft. King conference, Harney stopped off at Indian Key for an historic chat with Dr. Perrine. Temporary nurseries of the Mexican plants were doing nicely on the keys. Nothing seems to have been said, however, about the doctor's clandestine and dangerous jaunts over to Cape Sable to prod the soil and set out seeds.

Among other varieties he had planted on these scalp-risking trips were date palms. There are date palms at the Cape today. They look old enough to have grown from the doctor's seeds.

As a result of Harney's bringing in the chiefs from the southern part of the peninsula, Gen. Macomb announced in May, 1839, that he had "terminated the war with the Seminoles, by an agreement entered into with Chitto-Tustenuggee, principal chief of the Seminoles, and successor to Arpeika, commonly called Sam Jones."

The deal was that the Indians would stay on a reservation roughly from below Pease Creek to the Shark River and east to the Kissimmee River and Lake Okeechobee. The area did not impinge on the land Perrine wanted at Cape Sable.

The Army, in turn, agreed to keep white settlers out of the reservation.

Most historians, however, overlook the next sequence.

Violent and influential citizens of Florida stormed. They wanted the Indians completely out of the Territory—brave, squaw and papoose.

One prominent Floridian wrote Secretary of War Poinsett, demanding whether the treaty were a permanent measure. Poinsett's reply signed the death warrant for Perrine. It almost wrote off Harney's scalp, too.

Poinsett said the deal was only temporary. The letter was made public. The war was on again.

But Harney didn't know it. He left Tampa to found a trading post on the Caloosahatchie River intended to supply Indians on the reservation. Just two hours *after* he sailed from Tampa the mail brought the news of Poinsett's double-crossing letter.

Before Harney got to the trading site, however, the Indians there knew of Poinsett's bad faith. In their friendly chats with Harney during the day, they concealed their knowledge, and he had no reason to suspect they were just acting.

But disillusioned with white men now—even with the trusted Harney—the Indians, led by Chekika, descended in the night. Harney and a few others escaped barefoot through the mangroves. The rest were murdered, mutilated and left to the buzzards. Harney made it to the coast and was picked up by a vessel a few days later.

He headed back to alert his men at Cape Florida, but not before he returned to the scene of the river-bank massacre and saw what the Indians had done to the bodies of his men. At Cape Sable, the vessel fell in with the fast schooner Charles Howe, named for its owner, the postmaster at Indian Key, who was a partner of Dr. Perrine.

Howe's schooner sped with the bad news to the soldiers at Cape Florida, while Harney sailed for Key Vacas to warn the settlers where the village of Marathon is now. Then he hurried on to warn the 75 souls at Indian Key.

Though Harney gave all the horrible details, they apparently made little impression on the residents of Indian Key. The Caloosahatchie seemed a long way off, a Perrine daughter wrote later, and the presence of the dashing Naval officers and marines on the ships attached to Indian Key gave them a false sense of security.

Besides, did not the commander of the establishment have a letter of instructions from Mr. Poinsett, himself, to be especially solicitous for Dr. Perrine and his family?

Whatever Dr. Perrine's own immediate reaction was to his talk with Harney in July, 1839, it did not alter the course of his determined plan to colonize Cape Sable. The Lord, with the aid of the U. S. Army and Navy, he felt certain, would see it through.

Green Grow the Monuments

Dr. Henry Perrine, for whom the village south of Miami was named, years ago attracted the attention of biographers.

The few records of his life were widely scattered. The biographers had a hard time.

As a result, he "was born" in four different places and "lies buried" in two others. Actually, he was born in Brooklyn, N. Y., in 1797.

He has thousands of monuments. But he is buried under none. His only formal memorial is in the graveyard in Palmyra, N. Y., the residence of his wife before and after their marriage. She is buried there.

But Perrine's bones are more than a thousand miles from there, somewhere under the sands of Lower Matecumbe Key. No one knows exactly where.

Nor does any one, apparently, know what Dr. Perrine looked like. Search, so far, has failed to reveal a portrait either on canvas or in words. But the kind of a man he was is clear—brilliant, energetic, foolhardy, courageous and stubbornly persevering.

In the Everglades National Park area history, he enacted a dramatic sequence. The wild sisals, or century plants, progeny of the ones he brought from Mexico, are green monuments throughout South Florida to him and to his great vision.

The course of his plan was watched with great interest in high places, for it had the blessing and the hopes of the mighty in the Nation's capital and in the lofty circles of science. Big names in private finance and enterprise kept an eye on it and planned to come in.

When last seen alive, Dr. Perrine was helping his wife and three children down a trapdoor into a water-filled cellar under his residence on the shore of Indian Key before daylight of August 7, 1840. Outside, the Indians were whooping.

For 13 years he had schemed to get to South Florida. The chain of events that brought him to Florida started with a dire accident. As a young doctor on the "western frontier" of Illinois, he specialized in treating ague, or malaria. Besides experimenting with quinine as a remedy, he was trying out arsenic.

One night he took a hurried draught of quinine before going out on a call. In the bottom of the glass happened to be the dregs of some arsenic. He nearly died. His health was so weakened that he couldn't take the rigors of a northern climate thereafter.

He obtained appointment as American Consul in the warm port of Campeche, Yucatan, Mexico. There wasn't much to keep him busy. In 1827, like all the consuls abroad, he received a routine circular asking that useful foreign plants be sent home. The circular had been issued regularly since George Washington's presidency— with negligible results.

But it fired Perrine with ideas. He turned botanist. He studied Mexican plants carefully. He discovered a species new to science, a valuable hemp plant he named *Agave sisalana*. It is in the botanies today, credited to him. It is the commonly-known century plant.

There was no government bureau concerned with the introduction or propagation of foreign plants. It would be years before President Lincoln would found even the beginnings of the Department of Agriculture.

Perrine's keen mind functioned as effectively in his lonely outpost as a whole bureau, albeit such moderns as Dr. David Fairchild and his colleagues are so widely credited with "originating" tropical plant introduction that Perrine has largely been overlooked.

He had virtually the whole idea in the early 1800's. Moreover, he planned and carried it out almost single-handed. When he had laboriously gathered his temperature and soil data, selected his plants and analyzed the economics of southern agriculture and population, then, however, he found plenty of supporters.

The great botanist, Dr. John Torrey, and the Secretary of War, the Secretary of State, the Secretary of the Treasury, the Governor of the Territory of Florida and many others endorsed his project.

He got no Federal money, however. From his skimpy salary as consul, he financed the collecting of plants in Campeche. He corresponded with every man of science and reliable intelligence he could find in the Caribbean and Florida area. They told him what they knew and dug up answers to his pointed questions.

Charles Howe, postmaster at Indian Key, helped especially. He carefully kept temperature records there and communicated them to Perrine. William A. Whitehead, mayor of Key West, reported data from there. Perrine astutely compared the botanical and meteorological facts of Yucatan, Cuba, Louisiana and South Florida. They all pointed to the tip of the Florida mainland as definitely tropical— the only such area in the United States.

In a document that was a masterpiece of science, statesmanship and political acumen, he petitioned Congress for a grant of land on the peninsula. As one of the most important statements in the history of the area, it sheds great light on South Florida's early status and on the character of the men who then controlled its destiny.

The whole Territory of Florida had been a headache to the

Mrs. Henry Perrine

Perrine house and escape tunnel to wharf

Sisal at Indian Key

Oliver Griswold

Perrine Memorial, Palmyra, N.Y.

Louise G. Dean

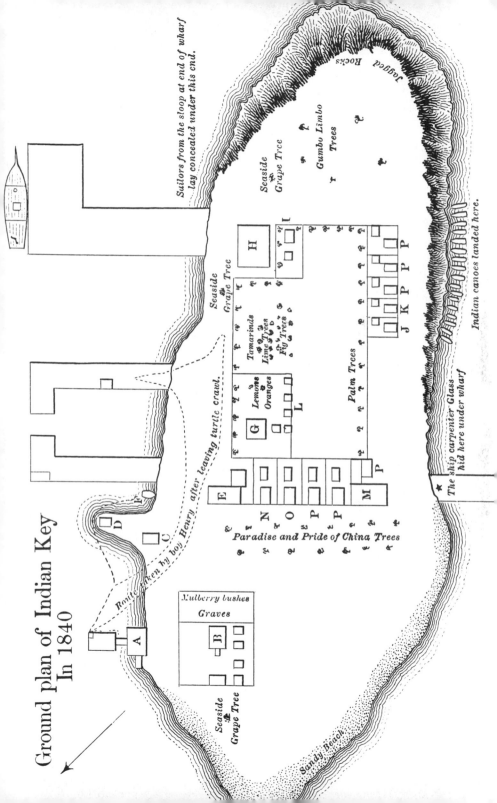

Ground plan of Indian Key
In 1840

Sailors from the sloop at end of wharf lay concealed under this end.

Jagged Rocks

Seaside Grape Tree

Gumbo Limbo Trees

Indian canoes landed here.

The ship carpenter Glass hid here under wharf.

H

I

J K P P P

Seaside Grape Tree

Tamarinds
Lime Trees
Fig Trees

Lemons & Oranges

G

L

Palm Trees

E

N O P P

M P

Paradise and Pride of China Trees

Route taken by boy Henry, after leaving turtle crawl.

D

C

Mulberry bushes

Graves

B

A

Seaside Grape Tree

Sandy Beach

The tall mangroves at Shark River

Oliver Griswold

owners of the five flags that had flown over it—the Spanish, the French, the British, the Republic of East Florida and the United States.

It was particularly painful to the U. S. body politic, at the time when Perrine sought his grant. The Second Seminole War was making a monkey of Uncle Sam. It was ludicrous, save for the blood and the cash it was costing.

Yet, the brass hats in Washington—and Perrine—were confident that the "slippery savages" would one day be quelled. Then what? Possibly only worse troubles of another sort. Perrine seemed to have a statesman-like solution.

Hitherto, South Florida had been considered too sickly and too sterile to merit the expense and trouble of surveying and selling. It was seriously contended that this section of the Territory was uninhabitable by whites and should, therefore, be abandoned to the savages and the runaway Negroes from the neighboring States.

The Senate Committee on Agriculture studied Perrine's enthusiastic plan and agreed that many millions of acres were "incapable of producing any article now cultivated in the United States" and must lie unemployed and useless for years, without some experiment such as he proposed.

Supported by the doctor's voluminous data on the new kinds of plants that could be grown in Florida, this argument was convincing. But probably the committee considered the following to be its punch paragraphs:

"When the Indians shall be expelled from the pestilential swamps and impenetrable morasses of southern Florida," the committee reported, "they may become again the impregnable fortresses for fugitive Negroes and piratical outlaws, who will be still more dangerous enemies to the tranquillity of our southern States than the actual savage Seminoles.

"But if the suggestions of the memorialist (Perrine), and if his experiments shall be successful, the arid sands and arid rocks, and mangrove thickets of the coast, the miry marshes, pestilential swamps, and impenetrable morasses of the interior, may all ultimately be covered by a dense population of small cultivators and of family manufacturers. Tropical Florida will thus form a well garrisoned bulwark against invasion in every shape and shade."

Congress granted the land, subject to Perrine's selection. Secretary of War Poinsett told him, that to protect him, he would make it a military post.

Just before Perrine and his family sailed from New York, however, Poinsett advised that the Indians had broken out again and there would be a delay in furnishing the military guard on the mainland.

Hence, the Perrines landed on Indian Key, Christmas morning,

1838, to wait out the final conquest of the Indians. But the intrepid doctor not only established various nurseries up and down the keys, but also went over to inspect Cape Sable and its environs, despite the Indian dangers. By July 4, 1840, he had selected his land.

He described his chosen Cape Sable tract as the "sheltered seashore of an ever-verdant prairie in a region of ever-blooming flowers, in an ever-frostless tropical Florida."

He was no longer relying only on Postmaster Howe's information. He had now explored it personally, the first man to view it with a scientific horticulturist's eye. Unquestionably he was also the first who saw it idealistically as the scene for a great development of unique national significance.

He wrote the General Land Office: "Have selected the site for said tract along the south coast of the peninsula, eastward of Cape Sable or of the projecting land called Punta Tancha on Spanish charts, and northward of the sandy islands of which one is called Cayo Axi on several charts. You are therefore requested to cause the Surveyor of Florida to survey said tract under my direction."

Robert Butler, surveyor general of the Territory, replied that he gravely doubted if he could find a surveyor willing to risk his scalp in that location.

Perrine was not discouraged. The schooner Medium was on that date anchored off Indian Key. It was loaded with canoes for the expedition that was to drive the Indians out of their last Everglades lairs. All the other Naval vessels were off, now, on a cruise to gather the latest information on the exact location of the Indian encampments.

They didn't know it, of course, nor did Dr. Perrine. But Chekika and his polyglot band of warriors, fugitive slaves and renegade Spaniards were lying in the jungle on Lower Matecumbe Key, less than a mile from the village on Indian Key, at that moment.

Indian Espionage

The scene of the historic South Florida drama of Indian Key is only a few minutes by skiff from the Overseas Highway between Upper and Lower Matecumbe Keys.

The little island first earned bloody repute several centuries ago. Some 400 Frenchmen were wrecked on nearby shores. The Caloosa Indians, who then held the Florida Keys, proved their reputed savagery by rounding them up on the little island and murdering them all.

Thereafter, in Spanish, the island bore the name Matanzas, or place of murder. The Indians used the island for a long time, then pirates, then wreckers. It was a busy salvage port when Dr. Perrine landed there.

From the highway today, you can see tall stalks rising from a wilderness of century plants. They are the offspring of those Dr. Perrine brought to the 11-acre islet from Yucatan.

Prone on the rocky shore was a great marble slab. It marked the grave of Capt. Housman, salvager, Indian trader and doughty speculator.

Among the thickets are the rock cisterns and brick foundations of the warehouses, a trading store, mechanical shops, dwellings and gun emplacements Housman built.

When Dr. Perrine and his family landed there Dec. 25, 1838, from New York, it was already a headquarters for operations against the Indians. Housman had disbanded the 24-man militia he had organized, when the U. S. revenue cutter Dexter arrived. Soon Commander Isaac Mayo, head of the Florida squadron, came on the steamer U.S.S. Poinsett. He reinforced the protection with a gun barge.

Later, in the spring of 1840, Lt. John T. McLaughlin set up a separate Naval station at Tea Table Key, less than a mile across the sparkling channel from the Perrine residence.

Indian Key was a bright little isle with streets and shady walks under beautiful trees, a delightful gem in a summer ocean. There was the Tropical Hotel erected by Housman for accommodation of transients and entertainment of the crews of wrecking vessels. His store did an annual trade of $30,000 some years.

The Naval vessels Wave and Flirt and others were based at

Tea Table Key. Fresh marines arrived to replenish the forces. The Army post at Cape Florida was re-energized.

The schooner Medium brought a load of canoes to carry the expeditions into the Everglades hide-outs and anchored off shore. The Wave and the Flirt and the rest went scouting in preparation for the final route of the savages from their lairs.

With all this action afoot, there was every reason for Dr. Perrine to believe that Secretary of War Poinsett's promise to make the mainland safe for his colony was about to be fulfilled. The redskins, obviously, were on the verge of annihilation.

On August 4, 1840, Dr. Perrine took his daughter Hester with him to Lower Matecumbe to inspect one of his nurseries of tropical plants. Down a path beneath the great jungle trees, he led her to a beautiful spring for a leisurely picnic lunch. The Indian war party, she learned later, was watching them all during the meal.

It had been several years since any Indians had been on Indian Key. A mysterious Spaniard had come by canoe some time before— to trade, he said. But Capt. Housman "obliged him to tell" that two Indians who had come with him were skulking on a nearby key. Captured as spies, they were turned over to the Dexter. They escaped. The historic conviction has been that they later guided Chekika's warriors to the massacre, advising where to lie in wait on Lower Matecumbe and when to time their strike.

The Indians knew when the Navy was away. They knew just where to land undetected. None of the village might have survived, had not a ship's carpenter, James Glass, been wakeful. Hester Perrine later said he found he couldn't get back to sleep and took his fowling piece to go around the shore to look for ducks. Rather unlikely—looking for ducks in August in the middle of the night. But it was a muggy, still night—hard on light sleepers.

When Glass discovered the empty canoes drawn up on the rocks in the starlight, he knew what they meant. Whispering, he wakened another carpenter, George F. Beiglet. They decided to try to make it across the island to Housman's. They hoped to distribute his arms and ammunition to the rest, before the Indians broke loose.

En route, they stumbled on the Indians. Glass fired. His shot and the resulting whoops and screeches roused the villagers—all 45 of them, 35 whites and 10 slaves.

The attackers went for Housman's residence first. He and his wife raced out the back door in their nightshirts, barefooted across the razor-edged coral and into the water. Their two pet dogs innocently barked in after them. Housman drowned them to hush them. He swam around to his dock, untied a boat, and he and his wife escaped to the Medium.

The Indians had a special interest in Housman. As much as his supplies, they wanted his detested skin.

They looted his house, his trading store, and his salvage warehouse. In addition to their big canoes, they even loaded his boats at his wharves and towed them away—a rich haul.

The Perrines dwelt in a house built by Charles Howe, the postmaster. It rested partly over the water. Underneath was a bathing cellar, refilled at every tide through a tunnel leading under the front porch and out under the wharf that extended from the porch steps.

Howe had originally built the tunnel to secrete an escape boat in the early days of the Indian scares. But when the Navy arrived, he barred off the outside exit of the tunnel and made a turtle pen under the end of the wharf.

As the Indians whooped in and out of Housman's residence, trying to find him, Dr. Perrine took one look out the window at the marauders. He hustled his family down the trapdoor into the cellar, dragged his chest of Mexican seeds over it to hide it, and went out on the upper porch.

He well knew that the Indians held a white physician in awe.

From the porch he delivered a talk in Spanish, telling them he would be glad to give them medicine later if they went away. They went.

This almost incredible scene was reported later by Hester Perrine and corroborated by the son, Henry E. Perrine, who heard all from their hiding place in the cellar. Months later, Indians who had taken part in the raid stated they had once intended to take the doctor alive. They wanted him, they confirmed, because they put much faith in the magic of a white medicine man, just as some whites thought there was magic in the remedies of Indian medicine men.

But the looters soon got into Housman's rum. Drunk and shrieking, they came back to the Perrine house, chased the doctor up into the cupola, smashed through the door and beat him to death. Maybe they were mad because they couldn't find Housman; maybe they were so drunk they thought Perrine *was* Housman.

They dumped the doctor's fine library out the upper windows into the water—and all his precious manuscripts.

They rifled the pantry. It was the day after baking day, and they gobbled cookies, cakes and tarts—then smashed all the crockery just for the fun of it. Leaving, they set fire to the house to force Mrs. Perrine and the children out of hiding.

Meanwhile, Midshipman Francis K. Murray, with a handful of sick men who had been left at the hospital on Tea Table Key, rowed over in a barge mounting four-pound swivel guns. By error, they overcharged the little cannon and blew them overboard. The Indians whooped in derision and replied with one of Housman's six-pounders. Murray had to retire.

Mrs. Perrine and Hester, Sarah and young Henry were at first almost choked to death by the smoke pouring through the tunnel from their blazing home. Then the wharf caught fire. They were nearly cooked.

It was long after daylight when the boy finally squeezed through the pilings blocking the exit of the tunnel, waded through the milling giant sea turtles confined under the wharf and climbed out.

A stack of cordwood on the end of the wharf had caught fire now. It looked as if it would be the pyre for his mother and sisters. It was about to plunge through on them.

Hysterically, he jumped into the water and floundered ashore. He saw no one except a boat load of Indians coming out from Upper Matecumbe, where they had taken the loot to repack it for the voyage to the mainland.

Suddenly his mother and sisters emerged through the wharf, their faces and shoulders seared. Their heads were plastered with marl they had scooped over their hair to keep it from catching fire.

They found a rowing launch partly loaded with loot. Sarah was weak from a recent illness. They hoisted her over the gunwales and shoved off, poling across the shallow flats toward the Medium.

Indians who had been loading the launch dashed out of the warehouse, yelling and shooting. The savages from Upper Matecumbe pursued. They gave up, however, when a boat set out from the schooner. It was rowed by dusky oarsmen. The Perrines headed out to sea. They thought the schooner had been captured and the oarsmen were Indians. But they were Negroes from the schooner's crew.

Aboard the Medium the Perrines found other survivors. Many others, too, were known to have hidden in cisterns and under buildings. They hoped to find the doctor safe among them.

As the last of the looters left Indian Key, they set fire to all but one of the important buildings. The black smoke plumes rose to stain the breezeless blue afternoon sky. Capt. Housman stood on the schooner deck, puffing a black "seegar," his arms folded disconsolately.

"There goes $200,000," he said.

When the villagers went ashore from the Medium, they found many other survivors. Among them was Henry Bateman Goodyear, brother of the inventor of rubber vulcanizing, who with Dr. Perrine had a significant interest in rubber possibilities at Cape Sable.

A boy named James Sturdy had been parboiled in a cistern under the burned warehouse. John Motte, his wife and two children, and a Negro child had been shot or beaten to death.

Mr. Howe helped the Perrine children look for their father. They found a thigh bone, a few ribs and a piece of skull in the ashes. They buried them under his favorite specimen of *Agave sisalana* in his nursery on Lower Matecumbe.

Long years after, the son came to take his father's remains North. He couldn't find them. The huge sisal had been swept away by a hurricane. The doctor's remains are still somewhere on the key.

Mr. Howe's house stood untouched. In their rummaging, the Indians had found his Masonic apron and other symbols. They spread them on a table and left.

Mrs. Perrine and the children were solicitously escorted North by an Army doctor. They wore oddments of clothes that had been contributed. That was all they had.

Harney's Hanging Party

Everybody in South Florida knew the massacre at Indian Key was important.

The terrible news reached the Army at Ft. Dallas at the mouth of the Miami River the next day, August 8, 1840.

The Navy came racing back from Key Biscayne to the scene of the disaster and immediately began writing embarrassed explanations of where it had been when the Indians descended. The settlers of all Florida were aghast.

The Indians were hardly out of sight with their loot, when the wreckers arrived by vessel from Key Largo. The news was sped to Key Vacas. The fleeing settlers took it on to Key West.

Sea captains carried dispatches from there to newspapers in the North—St. Augustine, Charleston, New York and Washington. The Key West paper interviewed survivors.

Major newspapers throughout the country mourned and snarled over the tragedy in black-bordered editorials. They demanded of the government why, even if it weren't smart enough to eradicate the few hundred remaining savages, it could not at least protect such an important figure as Dr. Henry Perrine. After all, he was residing less than a mile from a Naval station.

The Navy and the Army realized that they had a blunder to correct. Advised by an American-hating Spaniard, Chief Chekika, the 200-pound leader of the fierce Indians, had been the brains of the strategy. He was a bold and wily field commander.

The Indians had seized, not only a large supply of food, calico, linen and ready-made clothes, but tools, arms and four full kegs of powder.

That was a lot of powder. The savages could hold out, now, in their Big Cypress and Everglades fastnesses for a long time.

As Maj. Gen. Jesup had said, the whites knew as much about the inside of China as they did about the interior of the peninsula of South Florida. But the public uproar over the Indian Key holocaust decreed they had better find out and get busy. No more waiting on the perimeter to catch Indians when they came out. They must be ferreted out, no matter where, no matter how.

Numerous expeditions were planned. Lt. Col. Harney grinned when he got his orders. His assignment was Chekika—the devil who had routed Harney out of bed on the Caloosahatchie River and murdered his sleeping men. The indignity of having had to flee in his underwear and barefoot still rankled. He remembered the pain of the mangrove shoots on his feet.

Especially, he recalled how his dead dragoons had looked—face to the sky after the scalping knives and the buzzards had been at them. And poor widow Perrine and those lovely daughters and the fine son, having to accept charity from the good people of St. Augustine as they went North. And the great doctor himself, now a few scraps of bones in the sands of Lower Matecumbe.

It was worse, because Chekika had had the effrontery to kill a man who was front-page news. Professional and scientific societies and political clubs were passing and publishing resolutions of mourning and chagrin over the death of their brilliant colleague, Dr. Perrine.

Senators and Representatives in Washington were pounding the doors of the War Department, "demanding to know." They documented their ire with sheaves of the black-bordered press editorials.

Harney had the opportunity now to recoup, not only the honor of the War Department, but his own.

He vowed to do more. He would teach the Indians to fear him like the Evil Spirit, itself. As his steamer bore him south toward Cape Florida, it broke a shaft and put in to New Smyrna for repairs. Harney took the opportunity to buy from the captain of a fishing smack a coil of brand-new rope.

Among the heroes of the Seminole Wars were a few Negroes. Not all the slaves who ran away or were captured by the Indians were happy with them. Some watched their chance and escaped back to the whites. A few had been with the savages long enough to learn their language well. More important, they learned their strategy and the exact locations of their strongholds.

They became interpreters and guides for the military. One, who is identified in Harney's dispatches only as John, guided the expedition to Chekika's island.

Harney got 16 canoes from the Navy at Indian Key and started December 4, 1840, from Ft. Dallas for the headwaters of the Miami River. About 35 miles back of Coconut Grove, John reported, was Chekika.

Hidden in hammocks, or islands of higher land above the water and the vast stretches of saw grass, were Indian villages. On these very fertile rises, a growth of dense jungle screened the dwellers from outside view. Invaders would have to approach over miles of open saw grass.

Could white soldiers effect an undetected approach? Harney painted and dressed himself and his men to look like Indians. He taught them to paddle silently the 30-foot cypress log canoes. In a six-foot locker in the stern of each boat were rations of bread and meat. The ammunition was sealed from dampness in glass bottles.

The officer spread his blankets on the locker at night. The four or five men slept on their paddles and the thwarts.

The rainy season was over. But there was still water enough to float canoes over most of the route. When they grounded, the men jumped out in the mud and shoved—or hoisted them to their shoulders to portage the dry ridges.

Harney and the other officers shoved and hoisted, too.

The days were harmonious with the sweet songs of feathered choristers. The nights were loud and weird with the bellowing of alligators, the croaking of millions of frogs and the eerie symphony of myriad herons, ibises, spoonbills, water turkeys and limpkins.

In two days of excruciating travel they found no Indians— only one empty village. Then, one mid-day as the others rested, Harney called down from his look-out in a tree that two canoes of Indians were approaching.

He ordered Lt. Rankin to pursue. The Indians turned and raced off. The soldiers made their boats fairly fly in the chase. The Indians ran into the tall sawgrass. The soldiers fired. They winged two warriors and mortally wounded a squaw by accident. Altogether they got eight captives.

"The Colonel ordered ropes be made ready and we swung the two warriors to the top of a tall tree, where they hung darkly painted, against the crimson sky," a member of the expedition narrated.

Chekika's island was five miles farther on in the glades. That night was dark and rainy. The storm and the night cries of the birds would insure a stealthy approach. Lts. Rankin and Ord were sent ahead with an advance party to make the surprise. But it was after sunrise when they got there.

"But such was the confidence of the Indians in their own security, that our party was not discovered until they had crept up into their camp and commenced firing," a journal of the expedition recounts.

As the soldiers crept up, they heard wood-chopping. At the first volley, Chief Chekika, the chopper, threw down his axe and ran. He didn't have a chance—no more than Dr. Perrine in his cupola.

Chekika was wounded in the arm. Private Hall ran him down in the saw grass, finished him off with a shot, took his scalp and left the body.

Another warrior was killed and two warriors, a boy, five squaws, and some children were captured. Two other warriors escaped to an island four miles beyond. Lt. Ord and his men trailed them. The Indians raised a white flag. The soldiers halted. The Indians fired, wounding the officer and two men.

The troops couldn't return the fire. In wading they had splashed their guns. They fell back, waiting for Lt. Rankin and more men to come up for a charge. The Indians stood the assault coolly, holding it off to let squaws and children escape.

When Harney came up, the island was empty. Rankin pur-

54

sued the savages and got close enough to fire. Then the soldiers' boat tipped and their guns got wet, too.

Harney started out to get Chekika's body. He spied other Indians coming up a channel between the tall grasses and ambushed them. His captives included Chekika's mother, his wife, his child and his sister. They were paddling Harney's personal canoe, the one that had been taken by Chekika in the raid on the Caloosahatchie trading post.

"This evening, the Colonel had our two prisoners exalted to the top of one of the look-out trees, with the body of Chekika by their side," the describer of the expedition flatly reported.

Harney also had one of the Indian warriors witness this scene and kept him alive so he could tell other Indians about it later.

To the Indians this signified a critical change in Harney's attitude toward them. He had treated prisoners like honorable warriors before; now he hung them like dogs, they said, even degrading the chief by hanging his lifeless body.

The expedition recovered a large quantity of the plunder from Indian Key, but not all. Much had been distributed to other Indians in the Big Cypress country to the northwest.

Harney headed southwest through more unknown territory, from island hammock to island hammock. He flushed and killed a few more surprised warriors.

Like the rest, they had never dreamed the whites would dare, or be able, to penetrate the security of their peaceful Everglades. Harney trekked on to the Gulf—with his prisoners, the recovered plunder, a captured store of coonti flour and Chekika's scalp.

A little below the Ten Thousand Islands and a little above Cape Sable, he came down an unnamed river, today called the Harney River. He had been gone from Ft. Dallas 12 days.

By way of Indian Key, where the ashes of the Perrine residence had been cold, now, a little more than four months, he returned to Cape Florida to write his report.

In his account, told with official restraint, he omitted mention of hanging Chekika's body. Nor did he glorify the military significance of the expedition.

He left it for others to explain that he had broken the backbone of Indian resistance by surprising them in their last fastnesses. He had not only killed the most important Everglades chief and some of his best warriors, but had shattered the smug belief of the savages that they could hold out forever in the interior of the peninsula tip. The Indians never recovered from this psychological blow.

The mighty in Washington were pleased. The black-bordered editorials were answered. Chekika's scalp had been lifted. Perrine's death had been avenged.

The Captain Sneered at the Law

Of all the early characters who avidly reached for the riches of Cape Sable, the spiciest was Capt. Jacob Housman. He rose to be the first political boss of Dade County and he died at sea with his boots on.

His epitaph on a huge marble slab on Indian Key read: "To his friends he was sincere, to his enemies kind, and to all men faithful."

This utter fiction was prescribed by his widow, Elizabeth Ann, who, despite her connubial rhetoric, the courts shortly decreed had never been married to Housman.

In his youth, Housman was entrusted by his father to command a schooner hauling freight between the home port on Staten Island, N. Y., and nearby Long Island and Hudson River landings. Young Housman stole the vessel and headed for the West Indies.

He piled on the Florida Reef. Awaiting repairs in Key West, he observed the vastly lucrative industry of salvaging wrecked vessels and cargoes from the coral barrier in the early 1820's. Key West had already mushroomed into a bustling community, largely, because after the United States got Florida from Spain, American law gave wreckers a better deal than the Bahamas or Havana.

Housman, for all his youth, was packed with energy and man-sized nerve. With the vessel pirated from his father, he prospered at salvaging from the start. But his greedy vigor in horning in on the Key Westers soon had him in tangles.

Off Caesar's Creek, he found a French vessel bilged on the rocks and abandoned by her crew. He took off a sizable cargo of cochineal and logwood, much valued in Europe for dyes, and some sugar. Despite howls of Key Westers that he should submit the salvage to adjudication there, he sailed it to St. Augustine for decision.

The French consul shrieked "robbery" when Housman was awarded 95 per cent. Subsequent court wrangling finally gave him two thirds. Meanwhile, his Key West enemies published violent accusations for taking the cargo elsewhere. Sarcastically replying to "the impartial and disinterested conduct of the gentlemen of many avocations at Key West," he laid about him so vitriolically that forever after the embittered Key Westers campaigned for his downfall.

Whatever sympathy he may have merited at first as a newcomer, he soon lost. Consistently, he sneered at the law. Not that he was the only shady villain in the business. He was just the brassiest.

With the captain of a distressed ship he connived to split the salvage allowed on sale of the vessel and cargo, which included among other valuables, $32,000 in specie. They got away with it.

With part of his swag, Housman bought squatter's rights to Indian Key in 1825. The 11-acre islet, mostly of solid rock, halfway between Cape Florida and Key West, was a brilliant choice for his schemes.

A deep channel ran in from the sea between protecting shallow banks to provide a fine harbor. Housman quickly developed his port. He built good wharves, cut big storage cisterns in the rock, laid out streets and walks, erected a warehouse, blacksmith and carpenter shops, and a sizable retail store.

He filled a street with cottages for his clerks and carpenters. There were quarters for plenty of slaves. From lush jungles on nearby keys he transplanted full-sized palms and paradise trees. He brought load after load of topsoil to nourish pleasant gardens.

For himself he built a residence visitors described as an elegant mansion. For visiting officers, crews and passengers, he built the Tropical Hotel. Besides comfortable accommodations, it furnished nine-pins, billiards and beverages.

The government assigned as deputy customs inspector reliable Charles Howe.

A post office proclaimed that letters mailed to Indian Key would be distributed to New River, Cape Florida, Key Biscayne, Key Vacas and wrecking vessels of the reefs.

It was a beautiful, tight little isle—tight in the reins of Jacob Housman. Slave or free, most of the inhabitants worked for him. He controlled others through credit at his store. He used them for spies and witnesses at will. It was handy, indeed, virtually to direct the decisions of his salvage cases.

When Monroe County officials in Key West got nosey about the conduct of civil law, the Territorial Legislative Council suddenly created a new county with Indian Key as its seat. Housman's hand was obviously behind it. It removed from Monroe's jurisdiction all the keys east of Big Pine and a great domain on the mainland. That was in 1836.

In the new Dade County, there weren't enough men to form a grand and petit jury. Housman, already the plutocrat, was now also the autocrat.

Soon, he was licking his chops over a shipload of baled cotton that went aground on Pickles Reef. Housman rigged it with the captain to let two of his Indian Key minions arbitrate the value. They faithfully fixed him a delightful share. But the owners smelled fraud and proved it in court.

Meanwhile, Housman had sold the cotton for a fabulous profit. 'Twas but one example of the tricks he regularly worked. The fat income falling into his grasp, via arbitrations, phoney and otherwise, he converted into more wrecking ships and improvements at Indian Key.

When the Indians flared up on the mainland, he insured his investments by fortifying the key with breastworks and six and twelve-pound cannon. All able-bodied men, white and slave, he organized into a militia and armed them at his own expense, expecting to be reimbursed by the government. He never got it. They were, after all, mainly his employes protecting his property.

Then Housman salvaged a huge cargo from Carysfort Reef. The captain directed him to deliver it to Key West for salvage decision. Red-handed, Housman was caught diverting choicest items to his Indian Key warehouse. His arrogant avarice had been so consistently brazen in similar acts over the years that Judge James Webb of Superior Court gave him the worst.

He put him out of the wrecking business by revoking his license.

The population that had fled the Indians on the mainland, as well as the upper keys, had by now moved on down to Key West. Housman's retail business that once grossed $30,000 a year fell off. Dr. Perrine and his family, however, remained at Indian Key awaiting the end of Indian dangers before starting the doctor's proposed plant introduction plantation near Cape Sable.

The Navy established a station at nearby Tea Table Key. But this new business did not make up for that lost by the flight of most of the settlers. Advertisements for the Tropical Hotel as a health resort brought few guests.

Housman urged Congress to make Indian Key a full customs port of entry, hoping for some of the auction and trans-shipping business monopolized by Key West. In the confusing pros and cons of the arguments, Congress forgot about it.

Then Housman penned the incredible document proposing that the Federal Government contract to pay him $200 a head to catch or kill all the Indians in South Florida. Preposterous as the offer of one man to substitute for the whole Army and Navy might appear, the Territorial Council agreed, for reasons of its own, that "it offers the most economical and effective mode of ridding the country of these lawless banditti." It directed the delegate in Congress to urge the President to make the deal with Housman.

The proposal was read in Washington, but that was all Housman ever heard of that possible source of income. But the Indians heard of it, and Housman was marked for their special attention.

A lone Spaniard appeared at Indian Key. His offered explanation, as he carefully looked over the lay-out of the settlement, as we have previously noted, was that he had come to trade at the store. By what means he was made to talk is not recorded, but two skulking Indians who had come with him were soon combed out of the jungle of a nearby key.

They were locked up but, after several months, broke away.

The last of the Indians, with their allies, at this date had been pressed back into the Everglades. They were short of supplies for warfare, but long enough on memory to keep burning the grudge against Housman for his offer to eradicate them for $200 apiece.

The naval vessels, as we pointed out in an earlier chapter, were all away from Tea Table Key when some 125 or more Indians silently pulled up their long dugouts on the rocks of Indian Key before the dawn of August 7, 1840.

As they crashed in Housman's front door, he and Mrs. Housman sprinted through the back garden, out over the shore and escaped in a boat to the schooner Medium.

The savages, augmented by runaway slaves and Spanish freebooters, cleaned out the settlement, killed Dr. Perrine and six others. As they left, you will recall, they put the torch to the beautiful little isle.

Housman sued the government, for $144,000, contending that Indian Key itself was being used as a Naval station and, hence, the government was culpable for failing to protect him. This falsehood was shredded by the Congressional Committee of Claims, which added to its comment:

"We notice the remarkable fact that some $15,000 or $20,000 of this claim is for the *burning* of cisterns cut in solid rock of the island, and they filled with water at the time. True that climate has the warmth of a southern sun, but how this was done is not *perfectly plain* to this committee."

Housman didn't smile at the attempted joke. By the time the committee had gotten around to cracking it, he was seven years in his grave. Nor did it matter that his beautiful "Charleston bride" had been refused administration of his estate, because she couldn't show they were married.

Belatedly, too, it came to light that he tried to recoup his fortune by applying for a grant of land at Cape Sable. The terms of the request for the finest site there were so grandiose, 'tis difficult to measure what rapacious sins he plotted for the Cape.

He had really been finished off financially by the Indians. After the massacre he auctioned his remaining personal effects, his ships and his slaves. He was broke.

Without a wrecking license, he could only engage as an employee on a salvage craft. On May Day, 1841, in a heavy sea he attempted to board a wreck on the reefs.

Capt. Jacob Housman, he of the great agility, the proud and doughty mariner, slipped. He was crushed to death between the two heaving vessels.

A Martyr to Millinery

The grave of a courageous man lies at Cape Sable. The marker says simply:

GUY M. BRADLEY

1870-1905

FAITHFUL UNTO DEATH

---

*As Game Warden of Monroe County He Gave
His Life for the Cause to Which He Was Pledged*

He was a martyr to millinery, and his death spurred the conservation movement that resulted finally in the Everglades National Park.

Of all who have served in the great campaign to evolve the park, he is the only one to have the poignant honor of a last resting place on the scene.

The egrets of the Everglades had been shot off almost to extinction by 1900. Since 1870, the year Guy Bradley was born, the commercial killing for the hat trade had been steady and heavy. Many other species of Everglades birds were in danger, too.

William T. Dutcher, later president of the National Association of Audubon Societies, succeeded in 1901 in getting the Florida legislature to enact bird-protection laws. But the State had no funds for wardens.

To guard the major nesting rookeries of South Florida, the national Audubon organization raised money to employ four wardens. One of them was Bradley. Kirk Monroe, author and vice-president of the Florida (State) Audubon Society, had recommended him.

Bradley was appointed official county game warden in 1902 at the behest of the National Committee of Audubon Societies.

The rookeries in the Cape Sable area, including the famed Cuthbert rookery, were his charge. He was the son of E. R. Bradley, postmaster at the hamlet of Flamingo. The Bradleys were fine people. They were popular in Miami, where they had formerly lived, and they were popular in Flamingo. Mr. Bradley, senior, had gone there to be land agent for Henry M. Flagler's land company.

The Captain rests at Indian Key

Oliver Griswold

NOTE: The above photograph was taken in 1948. In the four years following, vandals had broken the slab in 23 pieces and innumerable chips. On August 2, 1952, The Historical Association of Southern Florida, with the permission of Dr. J. R. Williams, then owner of the Key, recovered the fragments and removed them to the association's vault in Coral Gables, pending restoration.

Great Egret in nuptial plummage by Audubon

*Historical Association of
Southern Florida*

Remains on Indian Key

Oliver Griswold

Guy M. Bradley's lonely grave

Oliver Griswold

Guy M. Bradley (from an old snapshot)

*Historical Association of
Southern Florida*

Tricolor Heron by Audubon

Flagler had once planned to build his Overseas Railroad Extension via Cape Sable to link Florida tracks with Cuba and South America by freight-car ferries. He changed the route to Key West. The Bradley's stayed on.

As a tolerable fiddle-player, 35-year-old Guy Bradley was a social asset to the isolated, frontier community. He was clean-cut and on his job reliable and courageous. His Audubon employers also esteemed his energy and conscientiousness.

When famed ornithologist Frank M. Chapman returned from touring the rookeries with Bradley in 1904, he told an interviewer for the New York Sun:

"That man Bradley is going to be killed sometime. He has been shot at more than once, and some day they are going to get him."

Despite the obvious dangers, Bradley kept on with his job. The last man from "the outside" to see Bradley alive was probably Sanford L. Cluett, vice president of Cluett, Peabody & Co., Troy, N. Y., who, on a trip to the Cape in 1905, discovered the then uncharted key now named for him. He had known Bradley since 1888 in Palm Beach.

Mr. Cluett wrote April 30, 1948, of a cruise to the Cape: "I spent several days there, and Guy told me of his connection with the Audubon Society—and further told me that he was going to arrest a poacher who was a dangerous character. This matter worried him very much, and he showed me his nickel-plated, I believe, 32 caliber pistol which he carried. I told him I thought it was altogether inadequate. We said good-bye when leaving there—in fact, he came out in his rowboat with his little boy to say farewell."

Everything that happened on July 8, 1905, will probably never be known exactly. Witnesses told their versions. Over the years, retelling by countless others has garbled and twisted the details, until oral versions current today bear little resemblance to the facts on record.

In Key West today, for example, you can hear "there was a rumor going 'round at the time" that the trouble did not start over bird killing. Capt. Walter Smith's house, the gossips say, had just been burned, and Bradley was suspected.

But the truth is that Bradley had been in his grave two weeks before the house was burned.

Newspapers in Key West, Palm Beach, and New York headlined the Bradley tragedy. The Miami Herald had not come into existence then. But in the Miami Morning News and the Miami Metropolis it was a big story.

Bradley had had trouble with Walter Smith and his sons before. They were habitual game violators, and Bradley had arrested Smith previously. Smith and his two sons, Tom and Dan, and two men named Baker and Eldridge, sailed off Flamingo in Smith's schooner to nearby Oyster Keys. Tom and Dan went in a skiff to the rookery on the keys. Soon the sounds of their shooting reached the shore.

Bradley started for the schooner in a skiff. Smith fired a shot in the air to summon his sons. They came out of the rookery with dead birds. Before Bradley arrived, they were aboard the schooner. When he approached, Smith asked him what he wanted.

"I want your son, Tom," Bradley said. Smith asked if he had a warrant.

"Some further talk ensued," the Miami Morning News recounted, "which ended by Smith shooting Bradley dead. Smith asserts Bradley fired first, and he fired in self-defense."

The shot struck Bradley in his left breast. Whether he died instantly or slowly will never be known, for according to the newspaper account, "Then Smith and his sons upsail and left for Key West, not even stopping to see if Bradley was dead or not, and leaving the body afloat in the skiff at the mercy of the wind and waves. Bradley's side of the case will never be told, and but little of it can be surmised."

In Key West, Smith pointed to a bullet hole in his mast. Whether Bradley or Smith actually put the hole there is an unanswered question.

S. L. Roberts, known in Flamingo as "Uncle Steve," testified that Smith had told him in April—three months before the shooting —"that Bradley had arrested him for shooting in the rookery and that he (Smith) had a Winchester rifle and that if Bradley ever attempted to arrest him again he would certainly kill the warden."

Smith was held in the Monroe County jail for the grand jury, in default of $5,000 bond.

Bradley's body was found the day after the shooting in his skiff near Sawfish Hole, close to East Cape. An inquest was held by Justice of the Peace Lowe, and the body was buried.

Meanwhile, Mr. and Mrs. Bradley, senior, were on a cruise in their sailboat visiting friends at Palm Beach. They reached Miami six days after their son's death, the day the Miami Metropolis printed the first account. They were tied up at the Hotel dock and didn't see the paper.

How they learned of Guy's death was told the next day by the Miami Morning News.

"It happened also," the paper said, "that they were close friends of Rev. E. V. Blackman, and when Mr. Blackman read the article in the Metropolis yesterday, he called at the boat to see Mr. and Mrs. Bradley. He showed them the item and it was the first they had heard of the trouble. They were engulfed in grief, and Mrs. Bradley was completely overcome. . . . Capt. George Meyers of the launch Clara has kindly consented to tow Mr. Bradley's boat to Flamingo."

The Palm Beach News said: "Surprise and sorrow struck all the older inhabitants of the Lake Worth section, when they heard of the shooting to death of Guy Bradley near his home at Flamingo by Capt. Smith. . . . It was a strange affair and possibly the end is not yet."

The National Association of Audubon Societies retained State Senator W. Hunt Harris of Key West and Col. J. T. Saunders of Miami to assist the State in the prosecution.

The story kept making headlines, even among such important events as: the Florida East Coast Railway was busy in Miami with preparations on the Overseas Extension to Key West. A large force of men was building an immense supply warehouse south of the terminal docks on the bay front.

Bids were opened for construction of the Long Key viaduct, the first of the great spans to link the keys.

The survey for draining the Everglades was finished.

Yellow fever had broken out in New Orleans. Florida was quarantined against New Orleans travellers. Commander Robert E. Peary, at the Grand Union Hotel, said the Peary Arctic Club needed $30,000 more to start for the North Pole.

Miami's highway link with the "outside world" was nearing completion; work on the last stretch to complete the road connection with Palm Beach was progressing rapidly between Ft. Lauderdale and Delray.

The papers headlined: "INDIGNANT NEIGHBORS BURN SMITH'S HOUSE — FLAMINGO PEOPLE INCENSED OVER KILLING OF GUY BRADLEY."

Dated from Key West, the article told: "the negro and his wife who were occupying Smith's house since he came here to give himself up, were ordered to move out, and as soon as they were out, the torch was applied and everything that would burn was destroyed.

"This act shows that the residents of Flamingo are indignant over the killing of Guy Bradley and that it would be unwise for Smith to return there, if he is released."

Five months after Smith had slain Bradley, he was released. Perhaps the Flamingo residents realized before they went to Key West to testify that they could give little helpful information and had applied what "Monroe County justice" they could by burning Smith's house before they went down to the hearing.

The grand jury sitting in the State Circuit Court at Key West "deemed the evidence of the State insufficient to bring the accused to trial and failed to present a true bill, the result being the same as an acquittal of the defendant."

Attorney Saunders said the State made a very weak case. The witnesses for the State could give no testimony of direct importance. All of Smith's witnesses—those who were with him on the schooner and the only ones who saw the shooting—swore Bradley shot first. No others could say they saw the tragedy. Consequently, the State failed in the prosecution.

"Every movement must have martyrs, and Guy Bradley is the first martyr to the cause of bird protection," President Dutcher of the National Association of Audubon Societies stated.

"A home is broken up, children left fatherless, their mother widowed, a faithful and devoted warden cut off in the movement. For what? That a few more plume birds might be secured to adorn heartless women's bonnets! Heretofore, the price has been the life of birds. Now human blood is added."

A marker for the grave of Bradley at Cape Sable was provided by the Florida (State) Audubon Society. The National Association bought Widow Bradley a cottage she selected in Key West. There she reared the two orphan sons.

Later, explorers found in the jungle on the shore of Seven Palm Lake another memorial. The trunk of a great, native royal palm bore the carefully carved inscription, "G. M. B., Jan. 31, 1901, 12 M., for F.E.C. Land Co."

Immediately aroused by the murder, public opinion was even more strongly in favor of bird protection. But public opinion did not reduce the risk for wardens in patrolling the wilderness rookeries. Three years after Bradley's murder Columbus G. McLeod, another Audubon warden, was killed in the Charlotte Harbor area.

The price of plumes was high. The birds were scarcer, and the poachers bolder. State laws, enforced only by the few men the Audubon funds could afford, were not the answer. Bradley's death taught the conservationists that.

If the great movement in the name of the bird painter and conservationist were to save the birds of the Everglades from extinction, something else was needed.

The Feather Fight

Nearly five years after the bullet-pierced body of Audubon Warden Guy M. Bradley had been cold in its grave at Cape Sable, and more than a thousand miles away, Charles Evans Hughes, Governor of New York State, poised his pen over the Audubon Plumage Bill.

Then he signed the historic act. It and subsequent laws, plus the watch by Audubon wardens over rookeries, saved the beautiful birds for the Everglades National Park.

That was in 1910. The law was a victorious climax in the bitter struggle for bird protection to which Guy Bradley was a martyr.

If people wondered what really was behind the Bradley murder, they knew by the time the Audubon Plumage Bill was passed in Albany. On the surface, the murder looked like the result of a simple personal conflict. Bradley, as Audubon warden protecting the plume-bearing birds in the Cape area, had tried to arrest a commercial bird shooter. He resisted and killed Bradley.

For a long time after, the National Association of Audubon Societies could not get men to take warden jobs. Some of the characters around the Cape were known to be tough. What made them so quick on the trigger, not only to kill birds, but to spill human blood?

It was not only at the Cape; other wardens were shot at elsewhere.

Two leading figures in conservation soon furnished the answer —Mr. Dutcher, first president of the National Audubon organization, and T. Gilbert Pearson, its astute, Florida-reared, Quaker legislative representative. They studied fundamental causes.

Milliners for years had played on the primitive desire of women for adornment. The tender-hearted sex, in large part, had thoughtlessly succumbed to the appeal of bird plumes—and even whole, stuffed birds—on their hats.

The millinery business made millions. Feathers were easy to use in obtaining highly ornamental effects. They came already designed in graceful forms.

They were already colored without the aid of man-made dyes. They came cheap—at first.

Then, as the craze for feathers was deftly promoted, great

demand reduced the supply. Prices to hunters went higher. They hunted harder, shot faster.

Pearson investigated all aspects of the business. He saw how the shooting was done in the Everglades and on the coast of the Carolinas. The traffic included, not only egrets, herons, and roseate spoonbills of Florida, but gulls and terns of the Atlantic coasts. Not only parts of birds, but whole ones, such as terns, were used in weighty hat decorations.

The shooting and shipping led mainly to one center—New York City. Though they made a good living, the plume hunters were small fry. The really fat profits were in the urban feather markets.

That the pretties for the hats cost the lives of birds, some of them by horrible, lingering death, the tradesmen naturally did not emphasize. That some species were on the verge of extinction was not a concern, except that being rarer, the price was higher and the profits greater.

The men and women who carried the wild life conservation banner in the name of Audubon wondered if the headquarters of destruction could be eradicated. Could this rich, entrenched business be declared illegal?

Was the feminine fascination for feathered adornment an inherent instinct or was it merely a trade-promoted fashion that could be changed for something less bloody?

Among the ardent supporters of the Audubon bird-protection program were many thoughtful women. The others, certainly, had never heard the facts.

Pearson and Dutcher—and many others—pioneers in the rising campaign for conservation of America's natural resources, stumped the lecture halls. With lantern slides they explained the value of birds—to farmers, to sportsmen, to nature-lovers, to humanitarians. They appealed on the basis of their economic value and to aesthetic appreciation of them as songsters and living embellishments in the out-of-doors.

They found, like nearly all who, before or since, have pleaded the cause of conservation, that many more people were in favor than against. As the campaign of education progressed, Pearson registered in Albany in January 1910 as lobbyist to put through the Audubon Plumage Bill.

The newspapers soon called the contest "the feather fight." It was a hearty clash, imbued, not only with emotions, but the action elements of first-class newspaper stories.

Assemblyman James Shea of Essex County introduced the bill. Assemblyman Alfred E. Smith headed the opposition in the lower chamber. Judge Julius Meyer represented the Eastern Millinery Association, and Benjamin Feiner, attorney, appeared for the Feather Importers Association of New York.

The kind of hokum the milliners had been giving women when they sold them the be-feathered bonnets was revealed in Feiner's contention that the egrets were not killed to get the feathers. The plumes were shed feathers that the hunters picked up under trees, he said.

The Audubon testimony, of course, was that the adult egrets were killed—and in the nesting season, when their lacey plumes were at their best. As a result, the nestlings died of slow starvation, and the species was rapidly nearing extinction by the most cruel methods. Plumes received by the feather dealers, with the birds' skin attached, were shown in proof.

An indication of the real basis of opposition to the legislation that would prohibit traffic in bird plumes came in the revelation of Allison Brothers, a firm of milliners, who reported that in a year they had sold $200,000 worth of egret plumes.

The bill, nevertheless, was reported favorably by the considering committee. Besides many news stories, it inspired an unusual editorial in the New York Times.

"What sane argument and good example cannot do to arouse women to a sense of bad taste and cruelty in wearing feathers and stuffed birds, the law cannot be expected to accomplish," the Times opined. Feiner sent a copy to each assemblyman.

The New York Mail published a story alleging that lobbyists and go betweens had spent $12,000 to defeat the bill and the feather trade was raising more.

When the bill came up for vote, Alfred E. Smith led the argument against it, contending it would destroy a great industry. It was alleged that 20,000 workers would be thrown out of employment and investments of $17,000,000 would be lost. Smith made one of his lowest scores. The bill won 108 to 15.

Next, the milliners worked on the senate. They made such statements as "I suggest every man who votes for such a bill be promptly boycotted by every woman of his acquaintance," and "I protest against any man's dictating in any way what any woman shall wear."

Attorney Feiner, in appearing before the senators, still stuck to his story that egret plumes were dropped feathers. Pearson again showed the scalps of egrets.

The bill was amended to allow milliners time to dispose of their stocks on hand, and the senate passed it. Only three dissented. The victory had cost a great deal; that is, for the thin treasury of the Audubon societies. There had been the salary of Pearson and travelling expenses. There had been some telegrams, and, of course, the life of Guy M. Bradley.

It was May 7, 1910, just five years less two months and a day, from the date Bradley had been sacrificed to Everglades bird protection, when Governor Hughes signed the bill.

Pearson recalled that Hughes asked only one question. It was about a recent U. S. Supreme Court decision upholding a similar Louisiana bill.

It had taken a long time to build up to this vital New York State act that struck at the heart of the Everglades feather trade. A few years later, the plume hunters had to be dealt with again. The price of egrets, now rarities in commerce, had gone up terrifically. They became worth twice their weight in gold in Europe. The hunters began smuggling them out of the Everglades, via Havana to London and Paris. They then came into New York as "imported."

It took more arduous work by Pearson, backed by Audubon society members and officials, to bring about Federal legislation. Customs laws soon prevented the importation.

Today, now that the cruel methods of obtaining egret plumes, not only in the United States, but in South America, are widely known, there is little demand in America.

The illegal hunting that persists in the Everglades today is mainly by local hunters for food and by a few visiting killers. The usual efficient curtailments are being applied by the National Park Service, the U. S. Fish and Wildlife Service, State wildlife officers, and the National Audubon Society.

They All Called It "Tropical"

At 10 a.m. on Dec. 15, 1930, Cape Sable and the rest of the Everglades National Park area reached a critical turning point in their history.

In the Capitol in Washington, the chairman of the House of Representatives Committee on Public Lands, the Hon. Don B. Colton, cleared his throat.

"Now, this bill has been introduced by Congressman Owen," he announced. "Mrs. Owen, we will be glad to have you take charge of the hearing in the presentation of your case here this morning."

Then, Congresswoman Ruth Bryan Owen of Coconut Grove astutely marshalled before the august committee a parade of authorities on the Everglades. The distinguished investigators had recently visited and appraised the area as a possible national park.

They comprised, not only the most renowned, but also the largest group of specialists to examine it up to that time—by blimp, by launch, by rowboat, by car, and on foot, they had explored it together.

Their report to Congress became one of the most delightful documents in the history of the area—colorful, enthusiastic, and conclusive. Instead of bearing the dead-pan title of "Hearings on H.R. 12381," it might well have been entitled "Cape Sable, We Love You."

Emphatically, they all called it tropical—as if each had made an original discovery. Of course, it is not—not in the geographical sense. Technically nothing north of the Tropic of Cancer is tropical.

Although Cape Sable is approximately 50 miles farther south than any other part of the U. S. mainland, its latitude of 25 degrees, 7 minutes, puts it in the North Temperate Zone.

But nature does not always adhere to man-made zones. John James Audubon, the bird painter and naturalist, from his observations of bird life there in 1832, called it tropical.

Dr. Henry Perrine, a few years later, collected the first substantial details on plant life and temperatures. Had the Congressmen of 1930 looked back in the records, they would have found Congress in 1838 using the Perrine data to call it "officially" tropical.

Perrine's descriptions of the Cape as an ever-frost-free land still stands. Warmed on three sides by the arc of the Gulf Stream and protected at the north by the sun-heated shallows of the Ever-

73

glades, not even the stiffest Northers have dropped its temperature below freezing.

Hence, orchids, brilliant tree-snails, and other tender forms of tropical plant and animal life burgeon in this protected isolation—the only spot of tropics on the U. S. mainland.

Early pioneers had always eyed its unique characteristics as something to exploit—for crops, for egret plumes, as a port, or for real estate. Later, a new type of explorer came—the scientists, who found in its lush variety a source for education and inspiration. Over the years, they wrote tomes. Usually they were a little breathless over their discoveries of tropical flora and fauna within the United States.

"Found nowhere else north of the Gulf Stream" is a frequent description.

In later years, they came not as individuals, but as representatives of great institutions—universities, museums, and government bureaus. For example, in contrast to Audubon was Arthur H. Howell, author of the 579-page work, "Florida Bird Life," published in 1930. During his 12 years of study in which he visited Cape Sable at various times, he was senior biologist of the U. S. Bureau of Biological Survey.

The men introduced by Congresswoman Owen to testify on the Everglades National Park bill had the benefit of many previous scientific investigations. It was their specific job, however, to interpret all the carefully-collected information in light of their own recent personal observations—and in terms Congress and the public could understand.

The first to speak was Horace M. Albright, director of the National Park Service. He spoke plainly.

"That Cape Sable area is one of the most beautiful places I have ever seen anywhere," he said. In the same vein, he went on. "It is a strange land, full of strange plants. There is an atmosphere of mystery and strangeness about the whole thing that attracts the attention of all who see the Everglades and will attract the multitude as much as a park like Yellowstone.

"We have been reading about the Everglades from the earliest days of geography study. The Everglades, like the big trees and the geysers, are in everybody's minds, and they should be given opportunity to see them."

His statement deserves an underscore in history. He was speaking, now at long last, on behalf of a new point of view. Whereas the pioneer had said, "I'll use it—use it up for its soil, for its creatures to eat and to wear on hats," Albright was saying. "Preserve it, preserve it for all the people of the United States."

And he was being seriously heard by Congressmen.

The party that accompanied Albright on the tour of inspection included men of high authority and keen intelligence. There was

E. H. Burlew, administrative assistant to the Secretary of Interior.

Dr. H. C. Bumpus of Brown University represented the Educational Committee of the National Park Service. Harlan P. Kelsey of the Southern Appalachian Park Commission; Roger W. Toll, superintendent of Yellowstone National Park, and A. B. Cammerer, associate director of the Park Service, contributed vast experience.

Dr. David Fairchild of Coconut Grove, formerly in charge of the U. S. Bureau of Foreign Plant Introduction, gave the benefit of his world-wide knowledge. Caspar Hodgson, head of the World Book Co., represented the Camp Fire Club of America and the National Parks Association. Dr. W. A. Clark of California, a lay authority on parks, also reported.

Dr. T. Gilbert Pearson, president of the National Association of Audubon Societies, was prominent in the group. He testified from his long and practical experience in protection of wildlife of the Everglades and the Cape.

Additional testifiers were John Kunkel Small, head curator of the New York Botanical Garden; Dr. Howard Kelly of Johns Hopkins University; Dr. Paul Bartsch, curator of mollusks, National Museum, Washington; and Ernest F. Coe, of Coconut Grove, chairman, the Tropic Everglades National Park Association.

They filled the record with facts and lists of Everglades birds, plants, insects, animals, reptiles, fish, and mollusks. They waxed eloquent with superlatives and pungent emphasis.

Few Congressmen ever received such a thorough and sprightly course in the natural history of any area. Through this audience of committeemen, the scientists knew, they were about to change the human history of the Everglades and Cape Sable. Their performance was historic and histrionic.

Dr. Kelly enlivened the meeting with a live, pet king snake, from which with remarkable showmanship he worked around to a convincing plea for the preservation of rare species of all creatures and swept on to a Chesterfieldian conclusion by presenting Mrs. Owen with a gorgeous collection of the brilliant ligui, or tree-snail, shells as a memento.

Dr. Bumpus dwelt on the wisdom of including examples of the entire range of U. S. natural history in the National Park system.

"I am not claiming that it is our purpose to educate the people who go into the parks," he said. "I do claim, however, that when visitors want substantial information concerning the behavior of nature, they are entitled to receive it.

"Furthermore, when a large, undeveloped area like the Everglades, possessing characteristics unrepresented in other parks and having educational values, is available for inclusion in the system, one's duty becomes clear.

"It is the more so, since the National Park system will be forever incomplete if this tropical area is not acquired."

Dr. Pearson cited seven specifications for a national park and added, "After we had been over this territory, we sat together one night and went over these in detail.

"It was the opinion of every member of the committee that the proposed Everglades Park area measures up 100 per cent to every one of these descriptions. The country is absolutely different from any other part of the Union."

Dr. Bartsch prefaced a lively talk on the ancient and modern geology of the tip of Florida with, "You have here trees which are draped and covered with orchids, ferns, bromeliads, and moss to such an extent that the hanging gardens of the Sultan of Johore fall into insignificance in comparison. There is not a region in the world that I have visited that could compare with this lower point of Florida in floral aspect."

Mr. Kelsey was enthusiastic, because, "it is very remarkable as being the only land in America that is 'in the making.' Everywhere else, there is a breaking down, a washing away of our continent. Here there was once emergence, then submergence, and now emergence again. . . . The shoreline is creeping seaward by means of the great mangrove forests, so that here we see the remarkable spectacle of a land actually 'in the making,' of a continent 'in the making'."

The committee listened to the experts for several days—fascinated. For the grand finale to clinch the hearing, Congresswoman Owen gave them Ernest Coe. He rose to the occasion with a trip for the Congressmen—via lantern slides—around Cape Sable and through the glades. It was a brilliant collection of scenes and creatures—breeze-swept beaches, deer, ibis, turkey, orchids, giant turtles, and Seminoles. Coe's soft voice provided effective accompaniment.

In significant conclusion, the chairman feelingly commented: "I do not know when I have attended a more interesting hearing."

Thereupon, the committee adjourned at 8:45, the night of Dec. 18, 1930. Seventy-eight pages of historic testimony were on the record, the basis for the 17 more years of campaigning to get the park established.

A depression and World War II intervened before the Florida legislature appropriated the necessary $2 million to purchase privately-owned lands within the designated park area and otherwise fulfilled requirements.

In the latter days of the term of the war-time Governor Spessard L. Holland, the movement was revived. On the urgent recommendation of John H. Baker, president of the National Audubon Society, whose wardens were still the faithful guardians of the great rookeries of the area, a new Everglades National Park Commission of 25 members was appointed by Governor Millard F. Caldwell in 1946. August Burghard of Ft. Lauderdale was made chairman.

Chairman of the commission's pivotal legislative committee was

John D. Pennekamp, associate editor of The Miami Herald. In less than a year, the required State legislation was passed. The money and the gift of approximately 800,000 acres of State-owned land constituted by far the largest contribution of any State for a national park.

In Dec. 1947—with fish fry, band music, a nation-wide radio hook-up, and the press of the Nation and thousands of citizens attending—President Harry S. Truman, at Everglades City, dedicated the park to the use of the People of the United States—forever.

Daniel B. Beard was appointed its first superintendent.

————o————

Epilogue

In the light of recent information and developments, two corrections to the chapter, "Many A Brave Ship," need to be made.

1) A photocopy of the *Journal of Their Majesties' Ship Winchester*, obtained from the Public Record Office in London, indicates that the vessel was not H.M.S., but rather T.M.S. Winchester. William and Mary reigned jointly in 1694 when the ship was built. Also, the loss of the ship was not due to a hurricane, although the weather was foul, but rather to a disease called scurvy. The sailing master recorded that only eight men were able to stand, not enough to take in sail when the ship struck the reef. Of the 350 men aboard at departure from Port Royal, Jamaica, many died and were buried at sea. The small rescue ship, sent in by the commodore of the squadron, removed about one hundred remaining sick men.

2) The English historian who wrote the account of Captain Jennings' raid on the Spanish salvors in 1716, quite probably confused the two great treasure fleet wrecks due to hurricanes: one in 1715 off Sebastian Inlet and the other in 1732 off Key Largo. Undoubtedly, Jennings' 1716 raid occurred at Sebastian, about 180 miles north of Key Largo.

Charles M. Brookfield
August 1985
Miami, Florida